HEAVEN
and HELL

*Biblical Teaching on
the Doctrines of*

HEAVEN
and HELL

Edward Donnelly

THE BANNER OF TRUTH TRUST

THE BANNER OF TRUTH TRUST
3 Murrayfield Road, Edinburgh EH12 6EL, UK
P O Box 621, Carlisle, PA 17013, USA

*

© Edward Donnelly 2001
Reprinted 2001
ISBN 0 85151 8117

*

Typeset in 11/13 pt Sabon MT at
the Banner of Truth Trust
Printed in Great Britain by
Bell & Bain Ltd.,
Glasgow

To Our Friends from the
Southeastern Family Conference
in Dayton, Tennessee,
with Love and Gratitude

Contents

I

Thinking the Unthinkable

Hell. What a ghastly subject! It has been called the ultimate horror of the universe. What sort of person would want to write on hell and who would be interested in reading about it? It seems a morbid, peculiar preoccupation, tending to confirm the suspicion that Christians are congenitally gloomy. Suppose an acquaintance were to ask 'What's that you have got?' as you read these pages. 'It's a book about hell', you reply. Would you find that embarrassing? It doesn't seem the best way to win friends and influence people. Do we really want to spend our time thinking about something so awful?

Hell certainly is an unpleasant topic and we are naturally reluctant to consider it. So many other truths of Scripture are intensely appealing. Studying them is a pleasure. They lift our spirits and we are eager to learn more. But to sit and reflect on the fate of the damned fills our hearts with heaviness. A sense of dread overcomes us, for the theme is sombre and terrible. Life is hard enough as it is. Why go out of our way to be depressed? We instinctively turn to more encouraging subjects.

So why should we think about hell? We need good reasons, for unless we are convinced that such a study will help us, we will have no appetite for it. We must be able to anticipate that this will strengthen us spiritually. We must be persuaded that neglecting this doctrine will endanger our own souls and the souls of generations to come.

Thinking about hell is important for three main reasons.

ITS INTRINSIC IMPORTANCE

The first reason is its intrinsic importance. Everything in the Bible is important, of course. But some truths are more vital than others. If we are ignorant of the fine points of the doctrine of angels, for example, or of some details of the Old Testament food laws, we will be the poorer. But we will not be damned. Other doctrines, however, are indispensable. Richard Baxter urged pastors to preach 'chiefly on the greatest, most certain, and most necessary truths'. 'Many other things', he says, 'are desirable to be known, but this must be known, or else our people are undone for ever.'[1] Hell is such a doctrine. It 'must be known'.

We can illustrate its importance in four ways.

The first is *the massive weight of biblical testimony*. Hell is not something referred to only occasionally in Scripture, in one or two obscure passages. On the contrary, extensive sections of the Word of God deal with this doctrine. The Bible refers more often to the wrath of God than to his love. The Old Testament is full of the Lord's fierce judgements on his enemies, foreshadowings of hell. Our Lord Jesus Christ had far more to say about hell than he did about heaven. That may seem surprising, but it is true. Christ was love incarnate, full of compassion and mercy and yet he speaks very frequently of judgement and of everlasting punishment. Even his title of 'Saviour' draws attention to hell. A saviour must save from something, and hell is the dreadful fate from which he rescues us. Towards the end of the book of Revelation, God is bringing to a close his written Word. It is striking that, along with reminders of the glories of heaven, the final pages of Scripture leave dread echoes in our consciousness: 'the bottomless pit . . . the lake which burns with fire and brimstone, which is the second death . . . outside' (*Rev.* 20:3; 21:8; 22:15). Now if God in his wisdom has chosen to provide us with so much information about hell, is it not obvious that it is hugely important? This alone would be reason enough to study it.

Secondly, it is intrinsically important because of *the content of the doctrine itself.* Hell is revealed as a place of torment where millions

---

[1] *The Reformed Pastor,* 1656; abridged edition, Edinburgh: Banner of Truth, 1974, p. 113.

of human beings will be enclosed forever. Statisticians tell us that approximately ninety-five million people die every year. That means that, every second, three human beings enter hell or heaven. Within the next hour, eleven thousand men, women and children will have gone forever to a place of everlasting joy or a place of everlasting pain. Imagine them dying even now, as you read these words – one, then another, then another. As you draw your next breath, several more are leaving this earth. When a plane crashes and two or three hundred people are suddenly snatched into eternity, everyone talks about it. It is an appalling disaster, headline news. We are grieved, our minds are full of what has happened. And yet eleven thousand of our fellow human beings, every hour of every day of the year, are reaching their eternal destination. Surely for this reason alone such a doctrine must be an important one.

Thirdly, *we are not remote from this catastrophe.* Someone has remarked that 'death is not a spectator sport'. Spectator sports do not involve us personally. We can look forward with immense interest and eagerness to a football or rugby match. We enjoy watching the skill of the players and are glad if 'our' team wins. But we will not be on the pitch and, in the long run, what happens does not really matter to us. No demands will be made upon our energy or ability. We run no risk of being injured. We are merely spectators. Yet this is not true of the doctrine of hell, for everyone by nature is heading towards that very place. It is not something that does not concern us. We have all sinned, we fall short of the glory of God, and the wages of sin is death. Each of us is going to die and after death we will face judgement. We are all, without exception, intimately involved.

You may think that some Bible doctrines do not apply to you directly. If you are not a parent, for example, you may feel that the biblical instructions to parents do not involve you. Or you may skip lightly over the teaching of the Word of God to employers, or to the rich, and so on. You may say, 'Well, it is interesting, it is true, but it does not immediately concern me.' That would be a mistake on your part, for 'all Scripture . . . is profitable' (2 *Tim.* 3:16), but it would be an understandable reaction. Yet not one of us can ever dare to say that about the doctrine of hell. It is the certain destiny of every unsaved sinner, and we are born sinners.

Finally, it is intrinsically important because *there is a way, but only one way, of escaping it*. We do not have a range of options. We cannot soothe our anxiety by imagining that many categories of people will not go there. We cannot say to ourselves, 'Well, hell is dreadful, hell is real. But after all, there are many ways of avoiding hell, so I don't need to be unduly concerned.' Scripture is clear. 'He who does not believe the Son shall not see life, but the wrath of God abides on him' (*John* 3:36). The only way to escape hell is through faith in Jesus Christ, the Son of God. Everyone else will be lost. Why should we think about hell? Because we are going there unless we take the one and only way of escape.

And there is a way. Hell is not inevitable. If it were, if there were no prospect of rescue, what point would there be in worrying about it? The most sensible course would be to dismiss it from our minds for as long as possible. But, because there is a sure and certain promise of help to all who want to be delivered from God's condemnation, nothing is more crucial than that we should pay this subject our closest attention. In the Bible, the way of salvation is made abundantly plain: 'For God so loved the world that He gave His only begotten Son, that whoever believes in Him should not perish but have everlasting life' (*John* 3:16).

Here, then, is our answer to those who would accuse us of being morbid and gloomy. Would they bring that same charge against a conference of doctors meeting to discuss cancer? Would they accuse them of being warped individuals, taking an unhealthy interest in something unpleasant? Of course not! We are thankful that physicians give their attention to these things, that they devote their skill and insight to dealing with such dreadful realities. Their purpose is to bring help and healing to many, and we would encourage them in this enterprise. Far from criticizing, we appreciate that they are studying disease not because they like to, but because it is a grim fact which needs to be faced. But hell is a far more terrible and more permanent reality. The most positive, loving, responsible thing we can do is to study that doctrine so that we may be better equipped to deliver others from such an unspeakably horrible place.

THE PERVASIVENESS OF UNBELIEF
The second reason for studying hell is the pervasiveness of unbelief

concerning it. If it were something universally accepted, if most people believed in hell and were accurately informed about it, we might not need to spend so much time considering it. But, in our generation, belief in hell has almost disappeared.

We can distinguish three levels of unbelief.

There is, first of all, *popular mockery*. Some years ago my wife and I attended a concert in a local school, where the children were performing little sketches and plays. It was a pleasant evening until, to our astonishment, a number of children appeared on the stage dressed as devils, with paper horns and tails. Marching round the platform, they sang a song about hell, where people 'frizzled and fried'. The audience laughed uproariously, while we sat with our flesh crawling. The words of Christ were an almost audible echo in our ears, 'Whoever causes one of these little ones . . . to sin, it would be better for him if a millstone were hung around his neck, and he were drowned in the depth of the sea' (*Matt.* 18:6). For most people, hell is a joke.

Or, at best, a useful advertising gimmick. In our newspapers and on our television screens, the damned are those who have to do without the product being promoted. Heaven is eating the bar of chocolate, wearing the perfume, driving the new car. On a recent trip in America we stopped at a visitor centre, where we picked up an advertisement for a restaurant, located in a building which had previously been a church. This had given the new owners an idea. Their brochure began, 'Regarding the food, it is so heavenly it must be sinful. Our chef uses the freshest ingredients available to produce soul-satisfying cuisine. Just as Eve tempted Adam, we are going to tempt you with today's dessert creations. Imagine a devilish chocolate ecstasy . . .' and so on. Then it ended 'Good cheer and God bless.' There is no need for further examples of these blasphemies. Hell is viewed as humorous and those who really believe in it are to be laughed at or avoided, preferably both. It is a matter of popular mockery.

Secondly, *hell is rejected by those who have given the matter serious thought*. For, amid all the froth and shallowness of popular culture, many people do think seriously. Those outside Christ are spiritually dead; they hate God; they are blind and their mental processes are distorted. All that is true. But among them are knowledgeable, thoughtful men and women who reflect deeply on important issues. To them, the idea of hell is morally disgusting and they are genuinely offended by it. They regard it as a primitive super-stition, a crude bogey-man used by a tyrannical church to terrify and manipulate its gullible adherents. The philosopher Bertrand Russell wrote, 'I do not myself feel that any person who is really profoundly humane can believe in everlasting punishment. It is a doctrine that put cruelty into the world and gave the world generations of cruel torture.'[1]

Many of those among whom we live and work will despise us for believing in hell. Wherever we turn in the modern world, we are surrounded by intelligent people who consider such a belief con-temptible or wicked. We will see later why they think this way. But we do need to realize how objectionable a teaching it is.

Thirdly, and most tragically and surprisingly, *this doctrine is being questioned by some evangelicals, who profess to believe in the Bible as the inspired Word of God.* We expect theological liberals to reject the idea of hell, and for a long time they have. But many leading evangelicals have now begun to challenge a doctrine which has been the unanimous belief of the Christian church for over nineteen hundred years. They are turning from orthodoxy to the teaching of annihilationism or 'conditional immortality', an assertion that only the righteous will live for ever and that God will at some stage allow the impenitent wicked to pass into nothingness.

This strange theory has entered the mainstream and is claiming parity of esteem at least with the traditional doctrine. In the United Kingdom, a recent influential report has concluded: 'We believe that the traditionalist-conditionalist debate on hell should be regarded as a secondary rather than a primary issue for evangelical theology.' It continues, 'We understand the current Evangelical Alliance Basis of Faith to allow both traditionalist and conditionalist interpretations

---

[1] Cited in Robert A. Peterson, *Hell on Trial: The Case for Eternal Punish-ment*, Phillipsburg, New Jersey: P & R Publishing, 1995, pp.4–5. This book and John Blanchard's *Whatever Happened to Hell?* (Darlington: Evangeli-cal Press, 1993) are the two finest modern treatments of hell. I am frequently indebted to them in the following pages.

of hell.'[1] John Stott has gone on record as questioning the orthodox view: 'The ultimate annihilation of the wicked should at least be accepted as a legitimate, biblically founded alternative to their eternal conscious torment.'[2] Philip Edgcumbe Hughes has come out strongly against the doctrine of eternal punishment: 'With the restoration of all things in the new heavens and the new earth . . . there will be no place for a second kingdom of darkness and death . . . When Christ fills all in all . . . how is it conceivable that there can be a section or realm of creation that does not belong to this fulness and by its very presence contradicts it?'[3] His view of the ultimate fate of the wicked is unambiguous: 'The destiny they have fashioned for themselves will cast them without hope into the abyss of obliteration.'[4] Other writers suggest a 'post-mortem evangelism', the idea that after death there will be an opportunity for faith for those who did not hear the gospel during their lifetime. Clark Pinnock has moved to what he calls 'inclusivism', the belief that God will forgive and receive to himself followers of other religions who have lived up to the light which they have been given.[5]

Not only do these men question hell, but some attack the biblical doctrine with an almost blasphemous vigour. John Wenham, a noted evangelical Greek and New Testament scholar, stated at a 1991 conference: 'I believe that endless torment is a hideous and unscriptural doctrine which has been a terrible burden on the mind of the church for many centuries and a blot on her presentation of the gospel. I should indeed be happy if before I die I could help in sweeping it away.'[6] Clark Pinnock goes even further: 'I consider the concept of hell as endless torment in body and mind an outrageous doctrine, a theological and moral enormity. How can Christians possibly

---

[1] *The Nature of Hell: A Report by the Evangelical Alliance Commission of Unity and Truth Among Evangelicals*, April 2000, cited in *Christianity Today*, 23 October 2000, p. 36.
[2] David L. Edwards and John Stott, *Essentials: A Liberal-Evangelical Dialogue*, London: Hodder & Stoughton, 1988, p. 320.
[3] *The True Image*, Grand Rapids: Eerdmans, 1989, p. 406.
[4] *Ibid.*, p. 407.
[5] See Peterson, *Hell on Trial*, pp. 150–2, 229–34.
[6] Cited in Blanchard, *Whatever Happened to Hell?*, p. 219.

project a deity of such cruelty and vindictiveness? Surely a God who would do such a thing is more like Satan than like God.'[1] To these men, everlasting torment is morally intolerable. It represents God as a monster, punishing his wretched victims with unending suffering.

In the face of such questioning and unbelief, it would be easy for the Lord's people to be swept away. They might be tempted to think, 'Well, these are clever men, great scholars, eminent leaders in the church, and hell is an unpleasant doctrine. Is it not possible that they are right? Perhaps new light has come to them, and we should follow their lead.'

Even where evangelicals hold to the doctrine, they tend to do so apologetically. Is the story true of the preacher who warned his listeners, 'Those who do not turn to Christ will suffer grave eschatological ramifications'? Factual or not, it encapsulates the timidity of much contemporary preaching. Modern volumes of evangelical theology devote few pages to the doctrine of hell. It is denied, watered down, ignored or treated as an embarrassing family secret, not to be mentioned in public.

Why should we think about hell? Because it is a very important doctrine. Because it is under savage and sustained attack from both the world and the professing church. Because here is where a battle is now raging. Martin Luther's definition of a good soldier was of a man who stood and fought where the struggle was fiercest. It is easy to be a soldier in peacetime, pleasant to parade up and down in a colourful uniform, waving a shiny weapon. Nor is it much of a hardship to stand guard at a quiet, secluded section of the battlefield. But in the blood and danger of the bitterest conflict is where the true warrior is proved.

There is a battle raging over this doctrine. It is being attacked by the devil. Skilful and persuasive men, some with a well-earned reputation for orthodoxy, are seeking to overthrow God's truth. That is reason enough for us to think about hell. We dare not run away. It is all too possible for doctrines to be lost for centuries. It has happened before. The gospel itself has been distorted and submerged. For hundreds of years, generations died in their sins because Christians had not fought for the truth. Do you want your children to

---

[1] Cited in Peterson, *Hell on Trial*, pp. 161.

grow up in a world where no one believes in hell and it is looked upon as a superstition of a past age? We have to know what we believe and why we believe it. We must be sure and firm and clear, so that we may do battle to keep this doctrine alive.

UNBELIEF AS A SYMPTOM OF A DEEPER PROBLEM

Why should we think about hell? Its intrinsic importance and the unbelief with which it is surrounded are both valid reasons. But there is a third, more significant than either of these. The unbelief is symptomatic of a deeper problem.

A symptom is so-called because it has an importance beyond itself. One day you discover a lump on your body. It is not painful and does not inconvenience you in any way. You can live normally and get on with your work. In that sense the lump is insignificant in and of itself. Yet is that how you react? Not if you care for your body and have any sense. You go to your doctor and have an examination. You seek treatment. It is not so much because of the lump, but because of what it might signify - something more dangerous, of which it could be an evidence.

Unbelief is, of course, more than a symptom. It is itself a sin. But the illustration is valid to this extent: unbelief is also an evidence of something worse. It is a symptom of humanity's deepest problem, man-centredness. Here is the root cause of all our difficulties. We make ourselves the centre of our universe. We become the beings around whom everything else revolves. It all goes back to Eden, where Satan said to Eve, 'You will be like God' (*Gen.* 3:5), and she listened. Indeed, it goes back further. Satan himself had said, 'I will be like the Most High' (*Isa.* 14:14).

This sin of self-centredness, or humanism (for that is another name for it), has been present in the world since the Fall. But it has in our day come to dominate the culture, so that it saturates the world in which we live. Man-centredness is as pervasive, and as unnoticed, as the air we breathe. No one is unaffected by it. Like pollution in the atmosphere, it is there, we absorb it, it is poisoning us.

Man-centredness is at the root of objections to hell, including the evangelical objections. The innovators tell us that their changed views are due to greater understanding. They have gone more deeply into the meaning of the original words, they have examined the background in the light of fresh knowledge, their exegetical skills are more precise than those of past generations. As a result, these more accurate methods of interpretation have led them inescapably to call into question the traditional doctrine of hell.

They may believe this to be the case, but it is not true. It is not an improved interpretative approach which has changed their thinking. It is the spirit of the world. Without realizing it, they have become affected by the man-centredness of our time, which has warped their judgment. They are emotionally averse to hell, but they have been clever enough to construct a persuasive rationale for conclusions which they reached irrationally. Their minds have been made up in advance and they have misused their exegetical abilities to enable them to arrive at a pre-determined conclusion. Truth is being abandoned, not because it is shown to be false but because it is felt to be unpopular and embarrassing. The change has come about 'not because of new light from the Bible but because of new darkness in the culture.'[1]

Let us look for a moment at three evidences of this spirit of humanism, noting how the doctrine of hell in each case opposes it.

It is shown firstly in *a man-centred view of man himself*. The highest imaginable value in our society is human well-being. This is the key, the purpose of all our activity, the foundation upon which our civilization is to be built. People must be happy.

But the doctrine of hell, like a brutal claw, rips its way through the fabric of that humanistic world view. For it tells us that millions of human beings will be unspeakably wretched for ever in a place of torment. Now, people cannot entertain this idea. They find it intolerable, for it calls into question everything modern man lives and stands for. Happiness is the chief good and man's well-being the goal. Millions of damned? No, no, they just will not accept that. They are emotionally prejudiced against it and their hearts persuade their minds towards unbelief.

Even Christians can be affected. Have you ever wondered how we can be happy in heaven if we know that other human beings are suffering in hell? For many this is an agonizing question, and we will

[1] Peterson, *Hell on Trial*, p. x.

return to it later on. But, for the moment, imagine yourself in heaven, beholding the glory of God. Jesus Christ, the Lamb slain for sinners, is there in all his beauty. You are surrounded by hosts of angels and the vast multitude of the redeemed. The new heaven and new earth lies before you in all its richness and wonder. Will you be unhappy? If being with Christ for ever is not enough for you, if you think that the damnation of sinners would spoil your joy in God's presence, is that not man-centredness? Is it not the influence of the world creeping in and affecting you? Yet, in our fallenness, in our self-absorption and self-importance, it is so natural for us to feel that way.

People have no difficulty with heaven, of course. Or, at least, with their distorted concept of heaven as a place designed purely for human happiness. Such a heaven is quite acceptable. It fits into their world view. But hell contradicts their comfortable assumption. It tears to pieces the man-centred view of man.

Secondly, *the world's view of sin is man-centred*. What is sin nowadays? It is not called 'sin', of course. But what is considered wrong or shameful? What sort of behaviour should we avoid? The best general answer might be that sin is anything that hurts others. We should try our best not to harm or cause distress to another person. That is seen to be evil.

Unfortunately, the criterion is selectively applied. There seems to be no problem about hurting those who are inconvenient or in the way. Unborn children are murdered in their millions. Our 'civilized' society does not mind driving scissors into the necks of babies in the womb, sucking out their brains and crushing their skulls. And if present trends continue, they will not mind eliminating the disabled or putting the elderly to sleep when they become too expensive to care for. We are heading for a world of horror, unless God in mercy turns our nations to himself.

Yet, however inconsistently, decent people do generally hold the view that we should not hurt others. We should not lie, exploit or use violence. Children should not be abused. Promises should not be broken. They agree with the sixth and eighth commandments: 'You shall not murder. You shall not steal', and, though to a rapidly decreasing extent, with the seventh: 'You shall not commit adultery'. They would be ashamed to do such things, or at any rate to be found out doing them. These commandments seem sensible rules for society. They know that the world would be a better place if such evils could be done away with and they are often troubled in their conscience if they cause hurt to others.

But try talking to them about the second, third and fourth commandments – not to worship God in any other way than that which is appointed in his Word, not to take God's name in vain, to keep the Sabbath day holy. These they regard as ridiculous. If, on a Lord's Day, you were to be tactless enough to approach your neighbour and point out, however graciously, that he should not be making repairs to his home or that she should not be going out to her keep-fit class, because these things are inconsistent with keeping the Sabbath holy, how would they respond? As well as becoming angry, they would think you were mad. 'What sort of religious freak are you?', they would retort. 'What harm am I doing? Who am I hurting?'

Why the difference? Why do people accept some of the commandments as valid, while rejecting others? Because they have a man-centred view of sin. Hurting people is wrong and they know that they should not do it. But they have no sense of sin as being against God. Commandments which seem to have no direct bearing on human welfare make no impact on their conscience. God simply does not matter. As far as guilt and wrong-doing are concerned, he can be left out of account.

But hell smashes this facade to pieces. Hell tells us that there is an awesome, holy God in whose eyes we are dreadfully guilty. This doctrine informs us that sin is so serious, so damnable in God's eyes, that it must be punished by an eternity of suffering. It lifts human wrongdoing to an entirely different plane and puts it in the context of accountability and judgement and everlasting consequences. Sin is not, first and foremost, hurting our fellow-humans. 'Sin is lawlessness' (*1 John* 3:4) and the broken law is God's. People do not want to hear about hell because it tells them that sin is more serious and more terrible than they have ever wanted to imagine. When a man who committed murder and adultery was convicted by the Holy Spirit, he did not in the first place lament the way in which he had hurt other people. Instead, he cried to God: 'Against You, You only, have I sinned, and done this evil in Your sight' (*Psa.* 51:4). Hell emphasizes that our sin has an eternal dimension as an affront to the Almighty.

Third, and worst of all, is *the man-centred view of God*. Have you noticed how our culture is systematically undermining all natural feelings of respect and admiration? We no longer have authentic heroes. People are celebrated for extravagant behaviour or conspicuous consumption, not for their value to society. Wealth is preferred to worth, glamour to virtue. There are many 'personalities', but few show evidence of character. Purity is sneered at. There is a prevailing mood of cynicism, a belief that no-one is noble or unselfish. The 'gutter press' ferrets out grubby secrets of the famous for the delight of their readers. Muck-raking biographers tear down the reputations of those about whom they write. No-one worthwhile is held up before us, no-one to challenge us to self-sacrifice or high endeavour. Everyone is dragged into the moral gutter with a knowing snigger. Heroes, it seems, are not popular. Why? Why this craze for reducing all to the lowest common denominator?

Because people hate *the* Hero, the Supreme Being. The world fears the thought of goodness and holiness standing in judgement over it. The God people speak about today – if he exists at all – is only for man's benefit. His purpose, it seems, is to supply our needs, to provide for our happiness. God is a heavenly bell-boy. When he is needed you ring for him, and when you don't need him any longer you tell him to go away. The first answer of the *Shorter Catechism* has been rewritten to read, 'God's chief end is to satisfy man and to provide for him forever'. Even in evangelical churches the impression is too often given that God exists to make us happy, to solve our problems, to answer our prayers, to heal our sicknesses, to improve our marriages, to help us to keep to a diet.

Luther described this as 'using God'. What a disgustingly accurate expression! Have you ever been used? You thought that someone was your friend. You assumed that they enjoyed your companionship and valued you for yourself. You trusted them, but then found out that they were using you. They cultivated you only for what they wanted from you, then laughed at you behind your back. What would you think of a man who spoke of using his wife? What a wretch he would be! Yet this is exactly what people are attempting to do with God. This is how they think they can treat the Lord of heaven and earth. There is no sense of his holiness, awesomeness or majesty. He is seen as a puppet who stays in a box until we press the switch to let him out.

But the doctrine of hell confronts us with a God who is over-whelming in his anger, irresistible in his power, terrifying in his justice. A mighty Sovereign, who holds the earth between his fingers like a pinch of dust. 'All the inhabitants of the earth are reputed as nothing; He does according to His will in the army of heaven and among the inhabitants of the earth. No one can restrain His hand or say to Him, "What have You done?"' (*Dan.* 4:35). Hell speaks to us of the God who is in control, doing with us as he pleases, the God whom we cannot ignore or marginalize or manipulate.

People today do not want a God like that, and they will banish any doctrine which brings him threateningly before them. This is why it is so vital that we think about hell. It brings us face to face with the living God. Here is a litmus test for our souls. Are you God-centred? Hell will test you.

But the converse is also true. If you are unsure about hell, God will convince you. Until people know God, they will not believe in hell. This doctrine cannot be taught in isolation. First we need to see God in his holiness and majesty, for, until we do, hell doesn't make sense. We cannot grasp it. This is why God-honouring churches and God-fearing Christians have such a vital ministry. Who else will tell of the great Lord Almighty?

But once we are confronted by the true God, once you and I gaze into the face of that majestic Being, then we are ready to believe all that God says. Doubters can raise their silly objections and offer their puerile questionings, but their basic problem is that they have never seen, or have for a time lost sight of, God as he is.

On the day of judgement no one will be laughing or producing flippant little brochures about heaven and hell. No one will be questioning the morality of eternal punishment. No broadminded preachers will be insisting, 'I don't believe a God of love could send anyone to hell.' We will all be ready to fall on our faces, overcome by the intense reality of the living God.

Why should we think about hell? Because it reminds us of our own littleness. Because it indicates graphically the awfulness of sin. Because it brings every one of us face to face with the overwhelming presence of God. That is why the devil has attacked this doctrine so persistently.

Some of you may still need to meet God. Face up, I urge you, to the reality of the God who made you and against whom you have sinned; the God to whom you are accountable; the God who will certainly condemn you if you do not cry to him for mercy; the God who will as certainly save all who believe in his Son.

Others of us, believers though we are, may have been influenced more than we realize by the thinking of the world. Our vision of God has grown dim and our faith has become too self-centred. 'What's in it for me?', we tend to ask. 'What about my wishes? Where do I fit in?' More than anything else we need to perceive our God again in his holiness and in his glory. May he use this doctrine to bring these realities before us.

And some of you live with a sorrow deeper than tears for loved ones who are now gone from this earth and who, as far as you know, had no interest in Christ. They were bone of your bone, flesh of your flesh. You loved them, you were right to love them, and the thought that they are lost brings unbearable pain. I cannot comfort you, but I can direct you to God. If you will come into his presence with your questions and your anguish, he will put his fatherly arms around you. You may not be given answers, but you will know the God of love, who cannot hurt any of his children, whose ways are altogether righteous, and your heart will be filled with his peace.

Remember the words of the redeemed in heaven, words which you will one day take as your own, 'We give You thanks, O Lord God Almighty . . . Because You have taken Your great power and reigned. The nations were angry, and Your wrath has come, and the time of the dead, that they should be judged . . . Great and marvellous are Your works, Lord God Almighty! Just and true are your ways, O King of the saints! Who shall not fear You, O Lord, and glorify Your name? For You alone are holy. For Your judgments have been manifested' (*Rev.* 11:17–18; 15:3–4).

This is the only answer, to see God. 'Blessed are those who mourn, For they shall be comforted . . . Blessed are the pure in heart, For they shall see God.'

2

Biblical Basics

SOME BIBLICAL DOCTRINES are particularly complex. Think, for example, of the Trinity – one God existing in three Persons: Father, Son and Holy Spirit. Who can begin to explain this mystery? Not even the mightiest human intellect is able to fathom such a concept. It is quite beyond our understanding.

Other teachings of Scripture are wonderfully unexpected. We could never have discovered them by our unaided reasoning. Had God not revealed them, they would have remained unknown. The supreme instance is, of course, the Father giving his Son for sinners. That the Lord himself should have become man, then lived, suffered and died in the place of his people is utterly astonishing. Not in a million years would any human have devised such a plan of salvation. It is unquestionably made in heaven, stamped indelibly with the hallmark of divinity.

The doctrine of hell is in neither of these categories.

Although there is much about it which we cannot understand, the basic idea is not, in itself, especially complex. Hell may be defined simply as the place of eternal conscious punishment for the wicked. This is straightforward enough. A child has no difficulty in grasping it.

Nor is hell something which would never have occurred to us apart from God's written revelation. Throughout history, people in almost every culture have had a sense of hell. Versions of hell are found in the other main world religions – Hinduism, Buddhism and Islam. An awareness of judgement to come seems part of our inheritance as beings made in God's image. Imprinted on human consciousness is the uneasy awareness that beyond this life is a place of punishment for those who do wrong. It is so often denied not because it is unreasonable but because it is extremely unwelcome.

In the New Testament church the doctrine of hell seems to have been one of the ABCs for new converts. The writer to the Hebrews refers to 'eternal judgment' as an 'elementary *principle* of Christ' (*Heb.* 6:1,2), in other words, foundational teaching introduced at the beginning of the Christian life. In our day, however, it has been neglected and we need to take time to clarify our understanding.

We can summarize the main aspects of the biblical doctrine of hell in five simple propositions. Then we will consider two difficulties which people often have with this teaching.

WHAT IS HELL?

A real place created by God

A popular contemporary idea of hell is that it is no more than a metaphor for the unhappiness we experience in this life. In the memorable words of French existentialist philosopher Jean-Paul Sartre, 'No need of brimstone or gridiron. Hell is other people.' For him, hell was the pain caused by the cruelty of our fellow human beings. People speak of devastating experiences as 'hellish'. 'I have been through hell', they say. Hell is seen as the dark side of life, the sadness and suffering through which people pass.

None of this is true. Hell is a real place. It is not a metaphor or a symbol, not a description of our inner desolation or our present sufferings, no matter how agonizing these may be. It is not a state of mind. It is a place, with spatial dimensions. In the parable of the rich man and Lazarus, the rich man speaks of 'this place of torment' (*Luke* 16:28), using the normal Greek word for 'place', from which our word 'topography' comes - the science of describing places. We are told that the doomed Judas Iscariot went 'to his own place' (*Acts* 1:25). We don't know where in the universe that place is, but it has a precise location somewhere. The Bible indicates its remoteness from God's life and light by describing it as 'out', 'outside', 'outer darkness'.

The most characteristic name for hell in the New Testament is *Gehenna*, a word with an interesting history. It referred to the valley of Hinnom, just outside Jerusalem, where the Israelites had burned their children in sacrifice to the Ammonite god Molech (2 *Chron.* 28:3; 33:6; 2 *Kings* 23:10). It was a place of devilment and heart-wrenching grief. By the first century this valley of Hinnom had become a rubbish dump, where offal was burned day and night. The people of Jesus' day associated it with smoke, stench and worms, all that was hideous and foul. This is the horribly vivid term chosen by our Lord as an appropriate picture of the real hell.

Because it is a place, it has been created by God. Since he created all things, and by his will they exist and were created (*Rev.* 4:11), the 'all things' must include hell. He brought it into being. It was by his command that everlasting fire was 'prepared for the devil and his angels' (*Matt.*25:41). We will see the significance of that later.

Just, terrible and everlasting punishment

Secondly, hell is a place of punishment. Is any idea more unpopular today? Not all kinds of punishment, of course. Remedial punishment, designed to make the offender a better person, is just about acceptable. The forces of political correctness have not yet managed to persuade governments to remove from parents the right to discipline children. The purpose of discipline is to teach them not to do wrong. Our hope is that our children will learn from this unpleasant experience and that we will not have to punish them again. The prison service follows the same philosophy, where the stated aim of imprisonment is the rehabilitation of the criminal. And some will admit a role for preventative punishment, employing it as a deterrent to keep others from committing the same offence and thus suffering a similar penalty. Such action serves as a warning flag to the community, and the correction of the guilty few is meant to ensure the continued obedience of the law-abiding many.

But the punishment which today's world will not tolerate is that which is retributive - punishment inflicted simply as recompense for evil done, because it is just that wrongdoers should suffer; punishment which marks abhorrence of wrong and commitment to right. Such punishment is regarded as barbaric and immoral. This is not because people have become more humane or civilized, but because they are frightened by a dark spectre. The shadow of hell haunts them. Disturbing whispers of judgement to come echo on the fringes of their consciousness. These intimations of God's wrath so terrify them that they will do all in their power to airbrush any idea of retributive punishment from our society. Like children hiding their heads under the bedclothes, they cower behind an assumed tender-heartedness so that the nightmare will go away. Perhaps they hope that if we abolish punishment, God will decide to do the same.

For punishment in hell is retributive. It is not remedial. It does not make anyone better. Purgatory, the idea that humans will be cleansed and improved through their sufferings after death, is a myth. The pains of hell are of absolutely no benefit to those who are being punished. Nor is such punishment preventative, except insofar as hearing of it now may turn people from sin to Christ. When God opens the judgement books and proclaims the final destiny of all, the punishment pronounced will be what people hate and fear above all: retributive punishment, imposed because wrong is wrong and God is against it. Our society shudders at that idea. It pierces hardened consciences and touches a deeply buried nerve of guilt.

This punishment will be just, because it is imposed by the holy Lord God, whose judgments are altogether true and righteous. Scripture tells us that, although all the ungodly will be punished, they will not all be punished to the same degree. Some will suffer more than others. The greater the guilt, the greater the penalty. God will deal with sins committed in ignorance less severely than with acts of conscious disobedience: 'That servant who knew his master's will, and did not . . . do according to his will, shall be beaten with many stripes. But he who did not know . . . shall be beaten with few. For everyone to whom much is given, from him much will be required; and to whom much has been committed, of him they will ask the more' (*Luke* 12:47–48).

Privileges neglected will increase the penalty received, for Christ gives a solemn warning to cities in Galilee where he had preached and performed miracles: 'Woe to you, Chorazin! Woe to you, Bethsaida! . . . it will be more tolerable for Tyre and Sidon . . . [and] for the land of Sodom in the day of judgment than for you' (*Matt.* 11:21–24). This must have been a staggering statement to those who first heard it. Respectable Galilean fishing villages more guilty in God's eyes than heathen Tyre or perverted Sodom! But such is the enormity of hearing and rejecting the Son of God. Scribes, who had unrivalled exposure to the Scriptures but who often proved hypocritical, greedy or dishonest, 'will receive greater condemnation' (*Mark* 12:38-40). Here is a sobering consideration for anyone brought up in a Christian home, but still uncommitted to the Saviour. The deepest pits of hell may well be reserved not for the notoriously wicked, but for those who, from childhood, were familiar with the message of salvation, yet never embraced it for themselves.

We are not told how the punishment will be graded. Perhaps God will inflict greater pain on some. Perhaps there will be a keener awareness of opportunities neglected, a deeper remorse. The worm of memory, a father's teaching or a mother's prayers, may be part of the torture of the damned in hell. The Bible does not tell us, and we must not speculate. But we do know that the punishment will be unchallengeably just. No one will ever be able to complain that it is not fair or that they have not deserved it. Hell is just.

It is also terrible, for it is a place of 'weeping and gnashing of teeth' (*Matt.* 8:12), where 'their worm does not die and the fire is not quenched' (*Mark* 9:44). Those in hell will 'drink of the wine of the wrath of God, which is poured out full strength into the cup of His indignation.' And they 'shall be tormented with fire and brimstone . . . And the smoke of their torment ascends forever and ever; and they have no rest day or night' (*Rev.* 14:10–11). This is no slap on the wrist. It is fearsome.

And it is everlasting. In spite of specious modern 'difficulties', the teaching of Scripture is crystal clear. We are told of 'everlasting destruction' (*2 Thess.* 1:9), 'everlasting fire . . . everlasting punishment' (*Matt.* 25:41,46), and in each case the same Greek word is used as that applied to 'everlasting' life. Just as the joys of heaven are eternal, so are the pains of hell. Jude speaks of 'the vengeance of eternal fire' (verse 7) and of 'the blackness of darkness forever' (verse 13).

How appalling this punishment will be – just, terrible and everlasting! John Calvin says, 'By such expressions the Holy Spirit certainly intended to confound all our senses with dread' (*Institutes*, III. xxv. 12).

For the devil, his angels and the unsaved

'All the interesting people will be in hell' wrote the Irish playwright, George Bernard Shaw, in a piece of flippant blasphemy. But that is not what the Bible tells us.

The devil will be in hell, 'cast into the lake of fire and brimstone' (*Rev.* 20:10). Accompanying him will be 'his angels' (*Matt.* 25:41), at present 'reserved in everlasting chains under darkness for the judgment of the great day' (*Jude* 6). These demons, already aware of their ultimate destiny when Jesus was on earth, cowered before the Saviour`s power: 'What have we to do with You? . . . Did You come to destroy us?' 'And they begged Him that He would not command them to go out into the abyss' (*Mark* 1:24; *Luke* 8:31).

Hell is also for the notoriously wicked. 'The cowardly, unbelieving, abominable, murderers, sexually immoral, sorcerers, idolaters and all liars shall have their part in the lake which burns with fire and brimstone' (*Rev.* 21:8). What a repellent rogues' gallery! These are George Bernard Shaw's 'interesting people'.

But it is not only the blatantly evil who will find themselves in hell. The apostle Paul identifies for us those on whom God will take vengeance 'in flaming fire'. Who are they? What monsters of depravity can they be? The Hitlers? the Stalins? Yes. But also all 'those who do not know God, and . . . who do not obey the gospel of our Lord Jesus Christ' (*2 Thess.* 1:8). Outwardly upright, decent people, many of them. Good citizens, caring parents, reliable employees, friendly neighbours. But they never trusted Christ as Saviour. They refused to 'obey the gospel'.

Are you in that position? You may think of yourself as a reasonably good person. You may feel that you are not guilty of any great crime, that you have never done anything of which you are really ashamed. But the gospel says, 'Believe on the Lord Jesus Christ', and you have not obeyed that command. Even if you were never to commit another sin, God will take vengeance in flaming fire upon you if you do not obey his gospel. Only those will escape hell who have trusted in Christ. 'He who does not believe the Son shall not see life, but the wrath of God abides on him' (*John* 3:36). But 'he who hears My word and believes in Him who sent Me has everlasting life, and shall not come into judgment, but has passed from death into life' (*John* 5:24).

The irrevocable destiny of the unbeliever at death

On the day of judgment, the bodies of unbelievers who have died will be raised from the grave, reunited with their souls and cast into hell. But we need to remember that their souls are in hell already. There is no no-man's-land in the universe, no waiting room between heaven and hell, no soul sleep or period of unconsciousness until the second coming of Christ. Souls which are not still inhabiting their bodies are either in heaven or in hell.

When believers die their souls go immediately to be with Christ. Paul wanted to 'depart and be with Christ, which is far better' (*Phil.* 1:23). The Saviour himself said to the dying thief, 'Today you will be with Me in Paradise' (*Luke* 23:43) and that is precisely what happens to every Christian at death. Conversely, when an unbeliever dies, he goes to be with Satan, which is far worse. As he passes from this earth, the devil whispers gloatingly, 'Today you will be with me in hell.' No other possibilities exist. Our souls will be with Christ or with Satan.

The Old Testament *Sheol* and the New Testament *Hades* have been taken by some to refer to a neutral, intermediate state, occupied by all humans before the return of Christ. But this is due to a misunderstanding, for these words are used in Scripture in at least two senses. They refer sometimes to the grave to which we all go and sometimes to the place of punishment to which believers do not go. The King James Version correctly varies its translation of *Sheol* according to the context, from 'grave' or 'pit' to 'hell'.

While Scripture has more to say about the destiny of believers than about that of the lost, its teaching is nonetheless quite plain regarding those who die without Christ. Our Lord's parable of the rich man and Lazarus clearly refers to the period before the general resurrection; the rich man has died and been buried, and his five brothers are still alive on the earth. The end of the world has not come. But, though dead, he is conscious, because 'being in torments in Hades he lifted up his eyes'. His body is decaying in the ground, but his soul is experiencing agony in hell. 'I am tormented', he cries, 'in this flame' (*Luke* 16:23–24).

All who have died in unbelief are suffering at this moment. 'The Lord knows how to deliver the godly out of temptations and to reserve the unjust under punishment (literally translated, 'to keep the unrighteous in a state of continuous punishment') for the day of judgment' (*2 Pet.* 2:9). There is no second chance, no future hope, no point in praying for the dead. They are beyond our prayers, which can no longer help them. Even Almighty God himself will not help them.

That is why the gospel is so urgent. That is why God calls on us to believe today, for once we die it is too late. The soul is, at that moment, irrevocably lost, awaiting only its reunion with the doomed body at the last day.

Ruled by God and existing for his glory

We need to emphasize that hell is ruled by God, for there is a popular idea that it is somehow outside his presence and reach. People think of hell as a kind of nuclear waste repository in which God will enclose the wicked. It will then be sealed, buried and forgotten about, and the souls in that dreadful place of torment will be left to their own devices. Perhaps John Milton, great Puritan though he was, is partly responsible for this misconception. In *Paradise Lost,* he devotes a great deal of attention to Satan, the chief angel. As the devil is about to enter hell, Milton makes him say, 'Here at least we shall be free . . . Here we may reign secure, and in my choice to reign is worth ambition, though in hell: Better to reign in hell than serve in heaven.'

The poet is giving him a ghastly kind of hope. 'Here we shall be free . . . we may reign secure'. Perhaps that is indeed what Satan thought and hoped for. 'I may be wretched, but I'll be my own master. This may be a place of misery, but at least I will be able to get away from God.' Many agree with him and see hell as the place where Satan reigns.

But it is not true. Hell is where God alone reigns. It is not an independent, self-contained demonic kingdom. God, who 'has power to cast into hell' (*Luke* 12:5), rules it and has prepared its fires (*Matt.* 25:41). He is present in hell, for the damned are tormented 'in the presence of the holy angels and in the presence of the Lamb' (*Rev.* 14:10). What an awful and mysterious statement! We will come back to it later.

No, the devil does not reign in hell. We must not represent him as a James Dean-type figure, a tragic, heroic rebel, who stands alone

and shakes his fist at God. Milton makes that mistake when he puts
the following words into Satan's mouth: 'What though the field be
lost? All is not lost; the unconquerable will . . . and courage never to
submit or yield: That glory never shall his wrath or might extort
from me. To bow and sue for grace with suppliant knee, and deify his
power . . . That were an ignominy and shame beneath this downfall.'

It strikes a chord deep inside us, doesn't it? Terrible though it may
be, there is something magnificent about an indomitable will, the
head which is bloody but unbowed, the spirit which cannot be
broken. Such defiance appeals to our arrogant fallen nature. But it
is bogus. 'At the name of Jesus every knee [shall] bow, of those in
heaven, and of those on earth, and of those under the earth, and
every tongue [shall] confess that Jesus Christ *is* Lord, to the glory of
God the Father' (*Phil.* 2:10). Satan will not be 'free', his will is not
'unconquerable', his 'courage' will be non-existent, his 'ignominy
and shame' total. 'All is' already 'lost'. He will not be a dark prince,
awesome in his wicked dignity, but a contemptible being, cowering
before the mighty King and Lord of all. God rules in hell as he rules
in heaven.

We must remember also that hell exists for God's glory. Properly
understood, it should not be an embarrassment to us. We need not
speak about it in whispers or wish that it did not exist. In hell, and
we can say this only in trembling reverence, God's glory will be un-
veiled in new and amazing ways. His kingly authority will be seen
more clearly than has ever been possible before. Fresh aspects of his
holiness and justice will be revealed to his wondering people.

We can dare to believe this because Scripture teaches it. The last
book of the Bible shows us the sinless inhabitants of heaven praising
and thanking God for hell. The twenty-four elders fall on their faces
before him, saying, 'We give you thanks, O Lord God Almighty . . .
because You have taken Your great power and reigned. The nations
were angry, and Your wrath has come, and the time of the dead that
they should be judged' (*Rev.* 11:17–18).

The angel of the waters praises the Lord for his judgments:
'You are righteous, O Lord . . . because You have judged these
things . . . and You have given them blood to drink. For it is their
just due' (*Rev.* 16:5–6). Like all else in creation, hell exists for
God's glory.

[24]

TWO DIFFICULTIES

Reasonably straightforward though these propositions may be, they do raise certain questions in our minds. Not all the problems which people have with the biblical doctrine of hell stem from unbelief or a reluctance to accept God's teaching. There are genuine difficulties with which godly men and women wrestle and which can cause them considerable distress. It may be helpful to look briefly at two of the most common.

Is hell disproportionately severe?

The first is this: are not the sufferings of hell, both in their duration and in their severity, disproportionate to the offences? Is it fair that human beings should be punished for their sins so dreadfully and for ever and ever? How can we avoid charging God with injustice here? Does the penalty not far outweigh the crime?

One answer is that we are in no position to criticize the penalty because we have little understanding of the extent of the guilt involved. Our concept of sin is utterly inadequate. Even the most sensitive conscience has little awareness of sin's true wickedness and we are simply not competent to assess how much punishment it deserves. We cannot appreciate how awful a thing it is to disobey God, nor are we able to weigh up the relative seriousness of our various offences against his law.

Contemporary society is in a state of ethical chaos. Imagine a group of young professionals enjoying a meal in any big-city restaurant. Not an eyebrow will be raised if someone mentions that they have recently had an abortion. A reference by another to their same-sex 'partner' will elicit no disapproval. But if one of the party were to light a cigarette in a no-smoking section of the restaurant? Shock, horror, unanimous disgust! Is exhaling tobacco smoke more reprehensible than sexual perversion or killing an unborn child? Are such people competent to make moral judgments, to decide how God should deal with sin? They cannot even distinguish between wickedness and bad manners.

The leaders of society, to take another example, generally disapprove of capital punishment – unless for an unusually serious crime. Normally they refuse to consider putting a human being to death, even for murder. But when a bomber kills hundreds in a city centre or on board a plane, or when a child is butchered in circumstances of revolting cruelty, some may be prepared to make an exception, to put their scruples to one side, because 'this, of course, is different, something really bad . . .'

Which is precisely the point: sin *is* really bad. It is the worst thing imaginable. A mortal being sets his or her will against the Creator. We refuse to worship him. We reject the authority of the Lord who made us. Sin is so serious because it is against God that it is directed, and the gravity of the offence depends on the dignity of the One against whom it is committed.

If we saw someone pulling a worm to pieces, we might be irritated at such a cruel, pointless way to treat a living creature. But we would not be appalled. We would not lie sleepless for hours, agonizing over its fate. If a cat were being mutilated, we would be much more upset and would probably intervene, because in our scale of values a cat is a nobler animal than a worm. And if we saw someone torturing a child, we would be horrified and the memory would stay with us for ever. In every case the action would be the same, but against a different kind of being. Cutting a worm in two is not as bad as cutting a human in two. But how serious, then, must be an offence against God, who is far above all creatures, the Creator, the Uncreated? How can we begin to measure such appalling wrongdoing?

Nor does the guilt of sin have any necessary connection with the time it takes to commit. People ask why they should be punished everlastingly for a sin which lasted for only a few hours or days. But their logic is faulty. You could murder someone in a second or defraud him of his life savings over a period of ten years. The first crime is 'shorter' than the second, but would it for that reason incur a lesser penalty? The amount of time is irrelevant to the guilt involved. Even a momentary sin has an eternal dimension, because it is against the God who is infinite.

We must remember, too, that those who are in hell continue to sin, incurring more guilt to all eternity. The divine sentence is, 'He who is unjust, let him be unjust still; he who is filthy, let him be filthy still' (*Rev.* 22:11). As John L. Dagg puts it, 'A sinner cannot become innocent by being confirmed in sin . . . The future condition of the wicked is chiefly terrible, because they are abandoned by God to the full exercise and influence of their unholy passions, and the consequent accumulation of guilt for ever and ever.'[1] In other words, those in hell become ever more guilty and accumulate ever more sin, which deserves increasing punishment. After countless ages, they have more to answer for than when they were first condemned.

But the ultimate proof of the seriousness of sin and the justice of everlasting punishment is provided by the cross of Christ. Listen to Dagg again: 'If wrath and damnation had been trivial matters, the sending of God's only Son into the world, the laying of our sins upon him, and the whole expedient adopted to deliver us from these inconsiderable evils would have been unworthy of infinite wisdom'. Do you see his argument? If sin is trivial, a comparatively small matter, would God have sent his Son to deal with it? If it is easily atoned for, if a light penalty is sufficient to make up for it, what a waste to pour out the precious blood of the Only Begotten! Dagg continues: 'The power of God's anger, finite intelligence cannot conceive; but God understands it well, and the full estimate of it was regarded in the deep counsels which devised the scheme of salvation.'[2] It is incredible that the all-wise Triune God would have devised and offered such a stupendous self-sacrifice in order to remove a merely finite evil. The death of Christ on Calvary is incompatible with a limited understanding of the guilt of sin. W. G. T. Shedd shows profound insight when he comments: 'The doctrine of Christ's vicarious atonement logically stands or falls with that of eternal punishment.'[3]

Let us be quite clear. If we lose hell, we will eventually lose the cross, for if there is no hell, there is no real point in the cross. Jesus did not need to come and be made a curse for sin. He did not need to enter the horror of forsakenness. The cross and hell stand or fall together. Hell is extreme, but that is because sin is extreme and because extreme measures were taken for our salvation. We cannot survey the wondrous cross, meditate on what the Saviour suffered and assert that hell is an inappropriate punishment for sin.

---

[1] *A Manual of Theology*, 1857, reprint, Harrisonburg, Va.: Sprinkle Publications, 1990, p. 373.

[2] *Ibid.*, pp. 365–6.

[3] *The Doctrine of Endless Punishment*, 1885, reprint, Edinburgh: Banner of Truth, 1986, p. 153.

But God is love. Is hell not contrary to the character of God?
This question presents another difficulty. God 'delights in mercy' (*Mic.* 7:18), so how can he bear to send some of his creatures to everlasting torment? Would you do that to a child, or even to a dog? Of course not. Not one of us would put an animal in the flames of hell forever. How then can God do it? Is he not a God of love?

Indeed he is. But he is also holy and just and his attributes fit harmoniously together. They do not oppose each other. God's love can never be set against his holiness, for these qualities are friends, not enemies. When he acts righteously, this does not compromise his mercy in any way. In the fullness of his perfection all his attributes are exercised and revealed without exception. None of them can be cancelled or overridden, for God cannot deny himself.

We would agree that it is right for the holy God to hate sin. This is an essential element in his being and, because he is infinite, he will hate sin with an infinite hatred. But if such hatred is good, should it not be expressed? God reveals his love and his grace, but he also displays his righteousness and his wrath. Not to do so would be to cripple himself and give us a partial picture of his glory. Yet there is no contradiction, for he is holy in his love and his kindness is not threatened by his justice.

Again, if challenged as to why a loving God does not simply overlook wrongdoing, we may ask if indifference to sin is a virtue? Do we admire people who have no clear sense of right and wrong? When a democracy is willing to elect unprincipled rascals to high office, what does that tell us about the nation's moral health? What would we think of someone who insisted on remaining close friends with an unrepentant child murderer or a judge who imposed the lightest possible sentence on such a criminal? Would we commend them for their kind-heartedness and good nature? Not at all. We would be sickened by their ethical insensitivity. We would despise or pity those who had so little distaste for wickedness. So why do people think that God should behave differently, that he should overlook evil in the interests of a genial benevolence?

Robert L. Dabney gives a powerful illustration from the experience of two people he knew. One was a saintly woman who trusted the Lord, lived a life of holiness and love, yet was plagued by pain and illness all her days and died in agony. The other was a wicked and immoral wretch, a cruel man who had committed murder. He spent his years in health and happiness and was taken from the world suddenly without an ache or pain. In Dabney's words:

> Now let us suppose that these two persons, appearing so nearly at the same time in the presence of God, were together introduced into the same heaven . . . If this is God's justice, then is He more fearful than blind chance, than the Prince of Darkness himself. To believe our everlasting destiny is in the hands of such unprincipled omnipotence, is more horrible than to dwell on the deceitful crust of a volcano.[1]

What sort of God would treat good and evil in the same way? If God could look at sin and say, 'It doesn't matter; it is of no real concern to me; forget about it, for I will; welcome to my heaven', he would be God no longer.

Or we could approach the problem by facing up to the obvious fact of the sufferings of this life. People ask how a God of love can inflict endless misery on his creatures. But we could equally ask how he can permit his creatures to suffer any misery at all. Yet he does. The world is full of pain and unhappiness. It is quite clear that God judges sin, and that he has done so since the Fall. We believe, however, that he is love, in spite of his judgments which foreshadow the future. As John Blanchard puts it: 'The judgments of God fall often enough in this world to let us know that God judges, but seldom enough to let us know that there must be a judgment to come.'[2]

If a loving God cannot inflict suffering, salvation would be automatic. If God were bound to forgive, if his love required him always to show mercy and to receive into heaven, then there would be no such thing as grace and we would not be indebted to him in any way. Redemption would be mandatory, our inalienable right. The cross would be a supreme irrelevance. If a God of love could not possibly send anyone to hell, then what would John 3:16 mean?

Unbelievers use hell to accuse God of a lack of love, a failure to be merciful. But the truth is that there is mercy. For in Christ 'God demonstrates His own love toward us, in that while we were still sinners, Christ died for us' (*Rom.* 5:8).

[1] *Systematic Theology*, 1871, reprint, Edinburgh: Banner of Truth, 1985, p. 861.
[2] *Whatever Happened to Hell?*, p. 101.

Sinners hear of the love of God; they are urged to accept his love. But if they reject and refuse it, and then complain that God is not loving, are they being reasonable? He is loving, but they do not want his love. They trample on it and then have the gall to criticize, to stand, as it were, at the foot of Calvary on which his only begotten Son bled and died and complain that they cannot believe in his mercy. How can anyone, in the light of the cross of Christ, dare to say that God is unloving?

To suggest that the existence of hell calls into question the love of the God and Father of our Lord Jesus is blasphemy.

The Purpose of the Biblical Doctrine

What we have been considering is undoubtedly disturbing. The Bible contains many statements about hell which are frightening in the extreme and for this it has been criticized as blood-thirsty and upsetting. Why, ask the critics, is it necessary for these grim ideas to be included in a religious book? Would it not be more appropriate for the Bible to be uniformly comforting and encouraging? Why has God revealed such a frightening doctrine in his Word? Who wants to read such stuff?

No-one, probably. But what we may want misses the point. I do not want to be wakened at three o'clock in the morning by someone bellowing 'Fire!' outside my bedroom window. I do not want to jump out of a warm bed, bang my leg on a chair in the darkness, scramble into a dressing-gown, rouse the whole family and stand with them in a cold street. If, on doing so, I were to discover that I had been the victim of a practical joke, I would be considerably annoyed and would think it a piece of irresponsible foolishness. If, however, I saw flames engulfing part of my house, I would instead be grateful to whoever had awakened me from sleep and saved our lives. The issue would not be the loud voice, the inconvenient hour, the frightening words or the upset and tension. The question would be, rather, Was the warning true? If so, then the louder the shouting, the better.

Warnings are unpleasant and, usually, unwelcome. But, if based on reality, they are loving and beneficial. We need them and should profit from them. God warns us, alarmingly, about hell because it is a frightening reality and he is urging us to escape it.

Suppose the Bible had told us nothing about hell, not a single word about future judgment and condemnation. Would that make it a more loving book? Is concealing unpleasant reality an evidence of true caring? Not at all, just the opposite. People complain about God's warnings when they should fall down on their knees and give thanks for them. It is in love and mercy that he warns us about hell, so that we may be delivered from it.

Jesus Christ has been described as the theologian of hell, because he has more to say about it than anyone else. But we can overlook what his emphasis on hell really implies. It certainly means that hell must be real, since our information about it comes from the lips of him who is 'the Truth'. But there is something even more wonderful.

In God's grace, the one who tells us most about hell is the only one who can save us from it. What more could we ask? The Person whom God sends to warn us is the very Person who can deliver us. That is the beauty and the marvel of God's warning. He sends the warning by means of the Deliverer. This is not a harsh, gloating message. It is infinitely kind and infused with hope.

You may have heard about hell on many occasions. Time and again you have been warned about the day of judgment and God's inevitable condemnation of sinners. But perhaps you have never yet turned to Christ, who alone can rescue you from this terrifying prospect. You have not repented of your sins. You have not called on the Lord Jesus to save you. His warnings have gone unheeded.

What will you say when you stand before God? He will remind you that you were warned, more than once. But you would not listen. You 'trampled the Son of God underfoot' and 'insulted the Spirit of grace' (*Heb.* 10:29). If you refuse to believe in Christ, if you will not receive him as your Saviour, you will be damned and you will deserve to be.

'Flee from the wrath to come' (*Matt.* 3:7).

3
Everlasting Destruction

CAN WE IMAGINE what being in hell will be like? Should we even try? Is there not something crass about attempting to picture the sufferings of the damned?

For, as far as many people are concerned, this is no academic exercise. The souls of their loved ones, who died without any evidence of saving faith, are probably in hell at this moment. Thinking about their present and future existence can only be intensely painful for those believers who cared for them. Would it not be better to draw a kindly veil over the destiny of the lost, to cloak the truth in a decent reticence? Perhaps some realities are just too appalling to contemplate.

We become even more reluctant to think and speak about hell when we observe the appalling insensitivity with which it has too often been described. One writer, for example, pictures the wicked 'hanging by their tongues while the flaming fire torments them from beneath.' Another says of someone in hell, 'The flames of fire gushed out from his ears and eyes and nostrils and at every pore.' The damned are described as eating each other, tearing each other with their teeth. In a particularly horrible passage from a nineteenth-century work, the tone is almost gloating: 'The little child is in this red-hot oven. Hear how it screams to come out. See how it turns and twists itself about in the fire. It beats its head against the roof of the oven and stamps its little feet on the floor.'[1] Bizarre statements like these go far beyond the sober truths of Scripture. They owe more to over-stimulated imaginations than to the teaching of the Holy Spirit. Such caricatures are crude, inaccurate and unbiblical. They embarrass us and we cringe at the thought of being associated with them.

Yet we must face up to the horror of hell's sufferings, for the Bible reveals them to us, vividly and at length. The Lord Jesus himself describes hell in detail and we are certainly not more sensitive or more tender of the sensibilities of God's people than he was. To claim that we are too refined and humane to consider such things would be to criticize our Saviour. He spoke graphically about what hell will be like and we should think about his words as seriously as we can.

What is important is to keep a firm rein on our imaginations, avoiding speculation and refusing to go beyond what the Word of God actually says. If we confine ourselves to the phrases and word-pictures found in Scripture, we will not go far wrong.

But this may raise a question in some minds. Is much of the language of the Bible not figurative and symbolic? Its human writers are fond of similes and metaphors. They express truth in colourful hyperbole, with the oriental love of emphasis by exaggeration. Do we not, then, need to be careful about interpreting descriptions of hell too literally? Poetic passages, for example, can become nonsensical if treated in this way. The point is a valid one. There are some statements about hell which we cannot interpret with a wooden lack of imagination. We are told, for example, that the devil is thrown into flames. But the devil is a spirit; he does not have a body. So, whatever these flames may be, we cannot restrict them to literal flames.

We also recognize that the reality of hell is so far beyond our experience that language cannot adequately describe it. That is true, indeed, about many things in life, often those which are most meaningful to us. Throughout history, poets and dramatists have ransacked their vocabularies in attempting to describe love. Their efforts have been magnificent, resulting in works of genius. But have they ever adequately told us what love is? Is there not so much more

---

[1] Quotations from Blanchard, *Whatever Happened to Hell?*, p. 124.

yet to be said? Or, on a less romantic level, how would you begin to explain, to someone who had never eaten it, the taste of your favourite food? Words are not enough. They can only go so far, painting pictures, but coming short of reality. John Calvin understood that hell was, literally, indescribable: 'Now, because no description can deal adequately with the gravity of God's vengeance against the wicked, their torments and tortures are figuratively expressed to us by physical things.'[1]

So we can agree that much of the language of Scripture is symbolic. But this leads many to the mistaken inference that behind these symbols there is no objective reality. These terrible expressions which the Bible uses about hell are, they say, just figures, pictures, not to be taken literally. We should not be alarmed by them, for hell, they claim, is not like this at all.

But that is a complete misunderstanding of what a symbol is. By its very nature a symbol or sign is always less than the reality it represents. The reality behind the symbol is always more. If we are driving along and see a sign on which two or three small children are pictured crossing the road, we know that there is a school nearby. But we do not imagine for a moment that the sign is a complete description of the school. The bread we eat at the Lord's table is a sign and seal of Jesus Christ. It is a marvellous symbol, speaking of the means of life, of humble faith, of personal receiving. But our Lord is infinitely more than this symbol of his body.

So there is no comfort to be found in saying that the language depicting hell is symbolic. That doesn't make hell any less dreadful. It reminds us, rather, that the reality is worse than the most terrifying of the symbols.

We want to try, for a short time, to imagine what being in hell will be like. If you are not a Christian, this concerns you urgently and directly, for if you do not trust in the Lord Jesus you will one day find yourself in hell. Then you will not have to imagine what it must be like, for you will know from experience. I pray that such will not be the case. May God the Holy Spirit work in your heart as you read these words so that this may be the time of your salvation, when Christ Jesus delivers you.

[1] *Institutes*, III.xxv.12.

We may summarize the Bible's teaching under four headings, considering hell as: absolute poverty, agonizing pain, an angry presence and an appalling prospect.

ABSOLUTE POVERTY

Firstly, hell is a place of absolute poverty, because it involves separation from God. The lost will be 'punished with everlasting destruction from the presence of the Lord' (*2 Thess.* 1:9). 'Depart from Me, you cursed', will be Christ's verdict on all those who are not his people (*Matt.* 25:41). He is banishing them, commanding them to go away from him. Perhaps this separation is why hell is so often referred to as a place of darkness. 'God is light and in him is no darkness at all' (*1 John* 1:5), but the wicked will be 'cast out into outer darkness' (*Matt.* 8:12). Going to hell means being separated from God.

You may not find that prospect troubling. You do not like thinking about God. He disturbs you. His existence is unwelcome and it would be a relief to be away from him for ever. You are quite happy now to live your life without reference to God and everlasting separation from him would be good news indeed. This is a common view, but it is based on a profound misunderstanding.

For no-one lives without God. No-one ever has or ever will. He gives you every breath you take. His kindness surrounds and sustains every moment of your existence. He makes his sun rise on both the evil and the good and sends rain on the unjust as well as on the just (*Matt.* 5:45). He gives you the beauty of a summer evening, the coolness of a refreshing breeze, the splendour of mountain scenery. He delights you with the taste of fresh crusty bread or the juice of a ripe peach.

Perhaps you have experienced the ecstasy of love. Your heart has melted in affection towards husband or wife, parents or children. Doubtless you have warmed yourself often at the glow of true friendship. These are God's gifts. You may appreciate art, literature or music. You may enjoy the exhilaration of sport and bodily exercise. You probably have ambitions in life, you may be fortunate enough to have work which challenges and satisfies you, projects or hobbies which you find stimulating. You laugh and feel happy. You lie down in bed at night and are restored by sleep. All of these are blessings from God. You are indebted to him for everything that makes life bearable and worthwhile.

But in hell all of this will be taken from you. Everyone you love, everything you value will be removed from your experience. No sun will shine. No flower will bloom. There will be no laughter, no excitement, no fulfilment of any kind. These things are from God and to be separated from him is to be separated from all his gifts. You take them for granted now; you never thank the Giver and you have no idea of the extent of your indebtedness to him. But, when they are taken away, what poverty!

More than that, in hell your very personality, the real 'you', will deteriorate for ever. All the dignity that you now have as an image bearer of God will be stripped from you. All your humanity will rot away, all your value will be lost. The key New Testament word here is 'destruction' or 'perishing'. This does not mean annihilation, but the ruin of all that is worthwhile. Something which perishes has become useless for its intended purpose, unrecognizable from what it once was. We speak of rubber 'perishing'. It may still be called rubber, but its elasticity and firmness have gone. It no longer possesses what provided its identity, it can no longer fulfil its true function. All that is left is a counterfeit.

To perish means that you, as a being, will become ever more degraded, more contemptible, more lonely. You will be surrounded by devils and by damned and wicked humans. They will hate you and you will hate them. Everything good in you will be taken away, and everything bad in you let loose. All your evil passions will burn, increasing and consuming you until you become utterly foul.

Such will be your existence. How wretched! Nothing good, nothing worthwhile, a horrible monotonous dreariness, unenlivened by a single ray of light as you fester and stew in your loathsomeness. That is what will happen to you. Think of the most hopeless derelict in the gutter. His existence is paradise compared with the poverty of hell.

AGONIZING PAIN

But there is something worse. Agonizing pain. The Bible most frequently describes hell as a place of fire. The wicked 'shall have their part in the lake which burns with fire' (*Rev.* 21:8). Our Lord warns us to amputate every occasion of sin from our lives because 'it is better for you to enter into life lame or maimed, rather than to be cast into the everlasting fire' (*Matt*. 18:8).

Why fire? One reason is that fire speaks of pain. The claim is made today that it refers primarily to annihilation. Hell is seen by some as an incinerator which reduces to nothingness whatever is put into it. But this does not square with the biblical evidence. The rich man in the parable asked for a drop of water on his tongue because, he said, 'I am tormented in this flame' (*Luke* 16:24). The fire did not annihilate. It caused pain. We are told that the idolater 'shall be tormented with fire and brimstone' (*Rev*. 14:10), and the verb used is the regular Greek term for 'to torture'. Fire tortures; it causes the most exquisite and intense agony.

Think of the pain of even the smallest burn. To touch a hot stove produces a blister which throbs for hours. A few drops of scalding water make us wince and cry out. Even a tiny spark stings and irritates. So what must be the pain of being cast into flames, body and soul, forever? We cannot imagine what it will mean for the resurrected bodies of the damned. We are not told how much of the suffering will be physical. But we can be sure that at the very least the fire of hell means excruciating agony. That is why the words are chosen. It will be a hideous counterpart of the bush that burned with fire but was not consumed (*Exod*. 3:2). The wicked will burn with fire but they will not be consumed.

Christ uses a particularly horrifying expression to describe hell when he refers to it as the place where 'their worm does not die and the fire is not quenched' (*Mark* 9:46). He is quoting the last verse of the book of Isaiah, where the prophet has been speaking of the new heavens and the new earth. God has gathered a great multitude from all nations to worship him in his temple. And the worshippers 'shall go forth and look upon the corpses of the men who have transgressed against Me. For their worm does not die, and their fire is not quenched' (*Isa*. 66:24). The reference is to corpses left unburied after battle, which was the greatest of disgraces in ancient times. To refuse honourable burial to an enemy was to inflict the ultimate humiliation. Conquerors who wished to degrade finally their lifeless foes would either burn their bodies or leave them to rot. But at least the fire went out when it had used up all its gruesome fuel. When the maggots had stripped the corpses to the bone, they died themselves. Here, however, the fire is never quenched and the worms are never satisfied. The Jews were so appalled by this prophecy that, most unusually, they transposed what are now verses 23 and 24 in their synagogue services, so that the public reading of Scripture would not end on such a ghastly note.

Yet this is the dreadful picture which our Lord applies to the torments of hell. The undying worm is something foul, endlessly gnawing at hell's inhabitants, eating at them continually, giving them no rest. This probably refers to conscience. We know something of the pain of conscience in this life. It can be terrible. An awareness of moral guilt can drive to madness or suicide. How many of those seeking therapy for stress or depression are really suffering from troubled consciences? They have sinned, yet know nothing of peace with God through Jesus Christ. They do not realize that what is disturbing them is a violated conscience. Stifled and abused, conscience is responsible for much of the internal unease which overshadows modern society.

Yet in this life our consciences are comparatively insensitive. Those of the ungodly, certainly, are often seared and callous. They do not register, as they should, the awfulness of sin. But it is very possible that in hell the consciences of the damned may be re-sensitized. John Flavel writes: 'Conscience, which should have been the sinner's curb on earth, becomes the whip that must lash his soul in hell. Neither is there any faculty or power belonging to the soul of man so fit and able to do it as his own conscience. That which was the seat and centre of all guilt, now becomes the seat and centre of all torments.' [1]

If you go to hell, how your conscience will reproach you! Perhaps you will remember your father leading your family in worship, reading the Bible and praying for you and with you. Or what about your mother, who told you about Jesus? She loved you and would have given anything to see you become a Christian. You will remember every church service you attended, every sermon you heard. You may recall occasions when Christ drew near, when your heart was moved and you knew that you should yield to the Saviour. Fine Christians will come to mind and the attractive example of

---

[1] 'A Treatise of the Soul of Man', *Works*, Vol. 3, reprint, London: Banner of Truth, 1968, pp.137–8.

godliness which they set before you. Or perhaps you did not have the benefit of a Christian background, and yet there have been times when you were frightened or in need and you promised to serve God if he helped you. He did, but your promises have remained unfulfilled. How will such memories appear to you in hell? Will they not be bitter? 'Why didn't I listen, why didn't I take advantage of all those opportunities?', you will cry. 'It is my own fault that I am here.' Your conscience will torment you. It will be an undying, voracious worm, allowing you no peace to all eternity.

And 'there will be weeping and gnashing of teeth' (*Matt.* 8:12). This is Christ's most frequent expression for the experience of hell (see, for example, *Matt.* 13:42; 22:13; 24:51; 25:30). 'Weeping.' How often in your life have you wept – really wept, with your heart breaking, feeling desolate, wretchedly unhappy, the grief swelling inside you like an aching weight until you thought that you must crumple or burst? You may have shed tears when you were misunderstood or betrayed or at times when you were unbearably lonely. Intense pain makes people weep. We have all cried bitterly over the death of someone we loved. That is the sort of sorrow described here, for the word which Jesus uses refers to loud wailing, an inconsolable misery.

Think of it! Jesus says that tears will pour down your cheeks in hell and that your body will be racked with uncontrollable sobbing. Sorrow of the most bitter kind will fill you, and not merely the sorrow of grief, but of guilt and of self-disgust. If all the tears shed on earth since Eden could be gathered together, they would not begin to compare with the tears of one individual in hell. You will weep far more than all the world has ever known. You will weep and weep for ever.

Not only will you weep, but there will be 'gnashing of teeth'. It sounds like rage or insanity. 'The wicked plots against the just, and gnashes at him with his teeth' (*Psa.* 37:12). The prophet describes how the enemies of Jerusalem 'have opened their mouth against you; they hiss and gnash their teeth' (*Lam.* 2:16). It is the picture of a rabid dog, fangs bared in mad anger. So the damned will be grinding their teeth in rage, in helpless anger at their companions, at themselves, at their sins, at God himself. The father of a demon-possessed boy described how, under the control of an evil spirit, 'he foams at the mouth, gnashes with his teeth' (*Mark* 9:18). That was a faint foreshadowing of the crazy fury of the lost.

Who can imagine the agony of hell? With our anaesthetics and analgesics of every description, we know little of pain in the modern world. But the torture of fire, the inner torment of a devouring worm, the enraged, bitter, sobbing of the damned – such will be the condition of everyone in hell. Is that what you will choose? Do you want to experience it for yourself?

Agonizing pain – could there be anything worse? Yes, indeed.

ANGRY PRESENCE

Because, thirdly, there is an angry presence. A commonly-held idea is that hell is the one place in the universe from which God is absent. This view finds typical expression in the well-known statement: 'Sin is man saying to God, Go away and leave me alone. Hell is God saying to man, You may have your wish.' It sounds neat, but could not be more mistaken. God is present everywhere, throughout all his creation, and hell is part of what he has created. The lost sinner will not be punished in some realm from which God has withdrawn, but will be 'tormented with fire and brimstone in the presence of the holy angels and in the presence of the Lamb' (*Rev.* 14:10). God is present in hell.

But is this not a contradiction? We have already seen that hell means separation from God. 'Depart from Me' will be the divine sentence pronounced upon the condemned (*Matt.* 7:23). They will be ordered to leave God, to go far away from him into outer darkness. So how can we speak of God's presence in the abode of those who have been separated from him?

The explanation is quite simple. Geographical distance has little to do with either closeness or separation. One of my best friends lives on the west coast of America, nearly seven thousand miles from my home. We are rarely able to spend time together, on three or four occasions perhaps in the past ten years. Yet, outside my family, there is no-one to whom I feel closer. We keep in touch, pray for each other, would turn instinctively to one another in a crisis. Whenever we do meet, we can pick up our friendship without dropping a beat. In spite of the distance between us, that is real intimacy.

On the other hand, I can remember all too vividly a married couple whom my wife and I counselled some years ago. Throughout the evening we spent talking in their home they sat beside one another, separated by only a few inches. Yet there might as well have been a continent between them. A deteriorating marriage had pushed them apart and their tense body language screamed mutual alienation. So corroded had the relationship become that the very presence of one was unbearably irritating to the other. They hated being together. Proximity was torture. We could sense what a relief it would be when we left and they could escape each other's company. Close? No, tragically and painfully distant.

This is what it means to be separated from God. It is a startling thought that everyone will spend eternity in God's immediate presence. But, when we think about it, this is the reality. God, who will be the heaven of one person, will be the hell of another. The damned are separated from God's grace and love and mercy. It is indeed true that between heaven and hell a great gulf is fixed. Yet God is close to those in hell, because he is present there in his anger. Hell is where God pours out his wrath on the condemned, not just in initial judgment, but for ever, personally and actively. Those who are in hell will see God in his holy fury. They will be compelled to gaze at their Judge, unable to shut their eyes. The sight of him, intolerably painful, will be their condemnation and their punishment.

It is fearful to reflect that unconverted men and women hate God in his goodness, for 'the carnal mind is enmity against God' (*Rom.* 8:7). But far more solemn is the realization that the Lord himself is the enemy of the ungodly. 'His soul hates' the wicked (*Psa.* 11:5), that is to say, he hates them with all of his being. And he will express that hatred with dreadful fierceness. 'I will act in fury', he says of idolatrous Judah. 'My eye will not spare nor will I have pity; and though they cry in My ears with a loud voice, I will not hear them' (*Ezek.* 8:18).

Nothing more terrible can be imagined. Indeed, 'It is a fearful thing to fall into the hands of the living God. For our God is a consuming fire' (*Heb.* 10:31; 12:29). The essence of the fire of hell is the anger of a holy God, the Lord's burning righteous rage. His 'fury is poured out like fire' (*Nahum* 1:6), a mighty release of wrath, unrestrained and indescribable. Unbelievers ridicule the idea of hell-fire. It seems to them absurdly melodramatic and 'over the top'. But they will change their minds. In hell they will no longer be laughing at literal flames. They will be longing for them. 'If only the punishment were boiling oil or blazing coal!', they will cry. 'If only it were as bearable as that!'

Here is the ultimate horror of hell; not the absolute poverty, not even the agonizing pain but the angry presence of God. The prophet asks a haunting and unanswerable question: 'Who among us shall dwell with the devouring fire? Who among us shall dwell with everlasting burnings?' (*Isa.* 33:14). And yet there is still another element in the punishment of sin.

APPALLING PROSPECT

For there is an appalling prospect; it will never end. The fire is everlasting, the punishment everlasting, the destruction an everlasting one (*Matt.* 18:8; 25:46; 2 *Thess.* 1:9). 'The smoke of their torment ascends forever and ever' (*Rev.* 14:11). 'They shall be tormented day and night forever and ever' (*Rev.* 20:10). The ultimate horror of hell is its everlastingness.

We cannot take it in. It is too huge. Just as we are unable to grasp what it means to be with God for ever, so we cannot understand eternal torment. Insomniacs are familiar with time's snail-like progress through a sleepless night. You try to rest, lying for hours with your eyes closed, then look at your watch and find that fifteen minutes have passed. You begin to wonder if a solar eclipse has blotted out the dawn. Morning, it seems, will never come. And when pain is added to sleeplessness, the hours of darkness appear so much longer. What must eternity in hell be like?

No-one has described this more powerfully than Jonathan Edwards in, for example, his mighty sermon *The Eternity of Hell Torments*. As he preached this message, some of his hearers were awakened to their danger and brought to saving faith. Let us listen for a moment as his voice leaps over the centuries and he preaches again:

> Consider what it is to suffer extreme torment for ever and ever; and to suffer it day and night, from one year to another, from one age to another, and from one thousand ages to another, and so adding age to

age, and thousands to thousands, in pain, in wailing and lamenting, groaning and shrieking, and gnashing your teeth; with your souls full of dreadful grief and amazement, your bodies full of racking torture, without any possibility of getting ease; without any possibility of moving God to pity by your cries; without any possibility of hiding yourselves from him; without any possibility of diverting your thoughts from your pain. Consider how dreadful despair will be in such torment; to know assuredly that you never, never shall be delivered from them; to have no hope: when you shall wish that you might be turned into nothing but shall have no hope of it . . . when you would rejoice, if you might but have any relief, after you have endured these torments millions of ages, but shall have no hope of it. After you shall have worn out the age of the sun, moon and stars . . . without rest day and night, or one minute's ease, yet you shall have no hope of ever being delivered; after you shall have worn a thousand more such ages you shall have no hope . . . but that still there are the same groans, the same shrieks, the same doleful cries, incessantly to be made by you, and that the smoke of your torment shall still ascend up for ever and ever.

The more the damned in hell think of the eternity of their torments, the more amazing will it appear to them; and alas! they will not be able to keep it out of their minds. Their tortures will not divert them from it, but will fix their attention to it. O how dreadful will eternity appear to them after they shall have been thinking on it for ages together, and shall have so long an experience of their torments! The damned in hell will have two infinites perpetually to amaze them and swallow them up; one is an infinite God, whose wrath they will bear and in whom they will behold their perfect and irreconcilable enemy. The other is the infinite duration of their torment.[1]

Unbelievers sometimes bluster about how, if necessary, they will cope with hell. John Stuart Mill said, 'I will call no being good, who is not what I mean when I apply that epithet to my fellow-creatures; and if such a being can sentence me to hell for not so calling him, to hell I will go.'[2] W. E. Henley's defiance has become the theme song of humanism:

[1] *Works,* vol. 2, 1843, reprint, Edinburgh: Banner of Truth, 1974, p. 88.
[2] Cited in Paul Helm, *The Last Things,* Edinburgh: Banner of Truth, 1989, p. 122.

My head is bloody, but unbowed . . .

It matters not how strait the gate,
How charged with punishments the scroll.
I am the master of my fate:
I am the captain of my soul.[1]

But this is no more than mindless bragging. Let the sinner pause at the gates of hell, muster all his strength and vigour, and summon up his resolution to bear what awaits him. Within half a second his courage will have melted away and he will be crying for mercy.

If you have not trusted Jesus Christ, and if you continue to reject him, this is what will happen to you. 'I can't bear it!', you will cry. But you will have to bear it, and for all eternity. It will go on and on for ever.

DON'T LISTEN TO THE DEVIL

Satan's goal is to lead you gently into hell and he is a master of the black arts of persuasion. If you have some knowledge of the Bible, he may adopt a theological approach, urging you to wait for a 'Damascus road' experience, some cataclysmic, irresistible intervention of God. Here is Satan the Bible student, persuading you to reason like this: 'God is sovereign, isn't he? He has his elect, none of whom will be lost. And no one can believe unless God gives them the ability to do so. Very well, then, if I am one of the elect, it is up to God to come down from heaven, stop me in my tracks and shake me into faith. When he does, I'll believe. Until that special moment, I'll continue as I am.'

Do you remember the rich man in the parable who wanted such a special moment for his unbelieving brothers? He asked, in fact, for a messenger to be sent to them from beyond the grave. 'I beg you, therefore, father, that you would send him to my father's house, for I have five brothers, that he may testify to them, lest they also come to this place of torment' (*Luke* 16:27,28). What a sensational evangelistic meeting that would have been! Imagine how dramatic would be the invitational brochure: 'Next week, at Bethany Reformed Church – Special Speaker, Direct from Eternity. One appearance only. Do not miss this visitor from the world to come!'

[1] From Henley's poem *Invictus*.

But Abraham's response was dismissively low-key: 'They have Moses and the prophets; let them hear them. If they do not hear Moses and the prophets, neither will they be persuaded though one rise from the dead' (*Luke* 16:29,31). You cannot depend for your conversion on extraordinary interventions by God. You do not need to, for he has provided in the Bible all the information you need for salvation. If you refuse to believe what he tells you, no sound and light display will change your destiny.

If you are still young, strong and healthy the devil may point to the absurdity of bothering now about death and judgment. Why, you have many years before you! Time enough when you are getting old. But how do you know you will live to be old? The Lord Jesus told of a man convinced that he had 'many years', who said to his soul, 'Take your ease; eat, drink and be merry. But God said to him, You fool! This night your soul will be required of you' (*Luke* 12:19,20). In Jonathan Edwards' memorable illustration, the wicked are like people walking over a pit on a rotten covering that is in many places too weak to bear their weight. They do not know, however, where the weak places are and every step is full of danger. At any moment your feet may slip through the fabric of time and you may fall into the world to come. God is keeping you alive even now and, if you are unconverted, he is as angry with you as with many in hell already. You will go to bed tonight in the hands of an angry God. What reason have you to think you will ever awake? And, if you do not, where will you be?

Perhaps you are afraid of being laughed at. You know that you ought to make your peace with God, but what about your friends? They are clever, sophisticated, flippant. You have heard, and probably joined in, their gibes at religion. What would they say if you became a Christian? Already you can hear the witticisms, see their expressions of pitying contempt. But will you allow other people to send you to hell? Will you let their laughter keep you from salvation? What a hideous parody of friendship! How many 'friends' will curse each other in the world to come? 'Christ came near to me', they will snarl, 'but I was thinking too much of your good opinion. You have ruined me. It's partly because of you that I am here'. And they will hate each other to all eternity. Damnation is too high a price to pay for friendship.

Or you may simply be in love with the pleasures of this sinful world and reluctant to give them up. There is a dreadful irony in Abraham's words to the rich man in hell: 'Son, remember that in your lifetime you received your good things' (*Luke* 16:25). 'Your good things'. How the phrase must have grated agonizingly on the soul of that damned, tormented being! 'My good things! Yes, I thought they were good things. I gave myself to them, to money and luxury and self-centredness. I valued them above everything else and for them I sold my immortal soul. But what do I think of these 'good things' now?'

There will be church-goers in hell. On the day of judgment, some preachers, evangelists and leaders will stand before Christ with expectant smiles on their faces, waiting to receive his 'Well done'. But to their astonishment and horror he will say, 'I never knew you. Depart from Me.' They may protest, 'Lord, Lord, have we not prophesied in Your name, cast out demons in Your name, and done many wonders in Your name? (*Matt.* 7:22-23). Surely we aren't going to hell?' But they will, for they were never born again, never made new people. Their faith was superficial and unreal.

Perhaps, even now, you disbelieve. You are not going to let a preacher frighten you with such a primitive bogey-man as this. You do not – and will not – accept that hell exists, or, if it does, that you will ever go there. That is certainly the majority viewpoint. In a recent Gallup poll in the United States no more than four percent of those questioned thought that they might end up in hell. Many lost souls once thought the same. They did not believe in hell. They believe now, for that is where they find themselves. But for them it is too late. For you it is not – yet. God is giving you an opportunity to escape by calling on his Son to be your Saviour.

What more can I say? You have seen from God's Word a little of what hell will be like. I cannot believe that you want to go there. But, if you do not cry to Christ to save you, that is the destiny which you are choosing for yourself. Are you really determined on such ruin?

And the most foolish aspect of it all is that your everlasting damnation is unnecessary. For the Lord Jesus Christ is pleading with you at this very moment. As you read these words, he is calling you to himself, commanding you to turn from the sin that brings only destruction. He is infinitely gracious and kind. If you ask him to be your Saviour, he will receive you and forgive you. He will wash you clean and make you safe for ever, and you will be holy and happy, looking forward to an eternity of joy and glory in heaven. 'Today, if you will hear his voice, Do not harden your hearts' (*Heb.* 4:7).

4

Hell and the Believer

JUST AS AN OUTBREAK OF FIRE in a building matters more to any who are trapped in the building than to those outside, so it is to unbelievers that the reality of hell should be of primary concern. For, if you have not yet repented of your sins and turned in faith to the Lord Jesus, hell is still your destiny. Unless you call on Christ to save you, you will experience its torments for yourself. How to escape damnation should be your number one priority.

But this does not mean that believers can forget about hell. It is true that we have been delivered from condemnation through faith in the Saviour. Those who trust in him will 'not perish but have everlasting life' (*John* 3:16). But the doctrine of hell, revealed in the Word of God, is intended to be permanently profitable for us, designed to promote our growth as Christians. The solemn reality of hell's existence cannot fail to influence us profoundly. It is simply not the case that, once we have been saved, we can put any thought of everlasting punishment to one side as no longer relevant. Instead we should ask the Holy Spirit to keep impressing hell deeply upon our redeemed consciousness. It is vital that we remain aware of it.

I can remember how reluctant I was when first asked to speak at a conference on this strand of the Bible's teaching and how miserable my studies initially made me. Who can think of the damnation of millions without sorrow? Yet, as I persevered, my feelings began to change. The heavy-heartedness was still there of course, but mixed to an increasing extent with awe and thankfulness. Now I am glad that I have learned a little bit more about hell. I hope and pray that it has changed me for the better.

There are many ways in which this doctrine should affect us, but we focus briefly on six.

PUTTING SIN TO DEATH

First, it should produce in us a daily commitment to putting sin to death. Our Lord himself makes this challenging application when he says to the disciples, 'If your right eye causes you to sin, pluck it out and cast it from you. If your right hand causes you to sin, cut it off and cast it from you; for it is more profitable for you that one of your members perish, than for your whole body to be cast into hell' (*Matt.* 5:29–30). Jesus is citing the doctrine of hell and bringing it to bear on the consciences of his followers. He is telling them, in effect, that dealing radically with personal sin is the only alternative to everlasting condemnation. 'Amputate your sin,' he says. 'Pluck it out, throw it away. If you do not, you will find yourself in hell'.

That may seem a strange statement for Christ to make. Is it not through faith in him that we are saved? The dying thief was hardly able to pluck out his right eye or cut off his right hand, yet Jesus assured him that, 'Today you will be with Me in Paradise' (*Luke* 23:43). When we come in trust to the Saviour are we not delivered from condemnation once and for all? Are not believers 'kept by the power of God through faith for salvation' to 'an inheritance . . . reserved in heaven' (*1 Pet.* 1:4,5)? Not one of his people will be lost, will they (*John* 17:12)? Where does this amputation come in? How is being 'cast into hell' a possibility for those who, once converted, are secure for ever?

Secure once converted, yes. But are they converted? Is their faith genuine? Time alone will tell. Believing in Jesus does deliver us from hell, but it is difficult in the early stages to distinguish true faith from false. Saving faith is the beginning of an ongoing relationship of trust. 'Believers' are men and women characterized by the daily exercise of belief. Those who have believed keep on believing. They depend on Christ today and will depend on him tomorrow in exactly the same way as they did when they were first saved. They continue to recognize their helplessness, to acknowledge and turn from their sin, to cast themselves afresh on Christ for mercy. Superficial faith, on the other hand, is an initial flame of enthusiasm which soon flickers and dies. Perseverance is the safest evidence of reality and of spiritual life.

And this is what Jesus is referring to when he contrasts hell with radical amputation of sin, for he is indicating that to fail to deal with our sins in this way is to show that we have never been converted at all. If you want to assure yourself that God has saved you from hell, then set to work killing your sins. Aim at a lifetime of conscious, scrupulous obedience. Determine in your heart to turn away from wrongdoing, to wrestle against temptation. Read the Bible, seek God in prayer, listen to the preaching of the Word, cultivate Christian fellowship. Avoid everything that takes you away from God. Make this your decided, permanent commitment and ask the Lord to help you. Plead with him: 'Turn away my eyes from looking at worthless things, and revive me in Your way' (*Psa.* 119:37). As you persevere by God's grace from day to day, the conviction will deepen in your heart that Christ is indeed your Saviour.

Our Lord is telling us that we are never to treat hell as irrelevant. The perseverance of the saints means persevering in repenting, persevering in believing, persevering in obeying. No matter how long you have been a professing Christian, the evidence that you are not going to hell is the way in which you deal with personal sin. In Paul's words, 'If by the Spirit you put to death the deeds of the body, you will live' (*Rom.* 8:13). John Owen expands on this process of putting sin to death and writes, 'Do you make it your daily work; be always at it whilst you live; cease not a day from this work; be killing sin or it will be killing you.'[1] Killing sin is a birthmark of the Christian.

It is a powerful motivation, is it not? Whenever you are tempted, when sin seems so compellingly attractive and the price of obedience so unpleasantly high, reflect on Matthew 5:29, 30. Remind yourself, 'If I go ahead and commit this sin, I am in fact telling the Lord that I want to go to hell.' How many times will a true believer say that to God? If the thought of hell does not stop you from sinning, you need to ask some basic questions about your spiritual state.

---

[1] 'On the Mortification of Sin in Believers', *Works*, reprint, London: Banner of Truth, 1967, Vol. 6, p. 9.

CONTENTMENT

Secondly, the doctrine of hell should produce in us a spirit of unbroken contentment, no matter what our circumstances may be. Paul, lying in prison and writing to friends who were anxious about his well-being, could testify that, 'I have learned in whatever state I am, to be content' (*Phil.* 4:11). It was a difficult lesson to absorb, but, although it had taken him time, he could finally say without affectation or pride, 'I have learned to be content. I have learned both to be full and to be hungry, both to abound and to suffer need' (*Phil.* 4:12). Can you say that you have learned to be content?

Many Christians have not. A Puritan pastor, Jeremiah Burroughs, comments that 'to be well skilled in the mystery of Christian contentment is the duty, glory and excellence of a Christian'. Duty, glory and excellence perhaps, and yet Burroughs, interestingly enough, entitled his book *The Rare Jewel of Christian Contentment.*[1] Jewels are rare, not commonplace, and contentment is a rare virtue and a mark of unusual grace.

It is easy, of course, to be contented when we are healthy, happy and prosperous, without a cloud on life's horizon. But when times are hard, when we are disappointed in ourselves and others, when we meet what used to be called God's 'frowning providences', then contentment is more elusive. The society in which we live does not encourage it. Capitalist economies keep buoyant by creating artificial discontent. Advertising is designed to make us dissatisfied with our car, our household appliances, our appearance, everything. Governments describe their citizens, with humiliating accuracy, as 'consumers'. What an elevating phrase! Pigs at a trough are consumers, and that, too often, is what we seem to be. It is hard to stay contented in an atmosphere of grasping envy.

Discontent delights the devil, for it is sin, one of the primal sins. Never was it more irrational than on the part of Adam and Eve. God had surrounded them with abundance and beauty in the garden of Eden. Everything that they could possibly need was provided for the taking. But they wanted more – and fell into ruin. It was, says Paul, the epitome of sin, when God's creatures 'did not glorify Him as God, nor were thankful' (*Rom.* 1:21). The dissatisfaction of the

[1] 1648; reprint, London: Banner of Truth, 1964, quotation from p. 19.

Israelites in the desert, when they protested about the manna and wished they were back in Egypt, angered God and led him to ask: 'How long shall I bear with this evil congregation who complain against Me?' (Num.14:27). Not only is discontent an offence to the Lord, but it robs us of happiness and peace of mind. It proves, moreover, a stumbling-block to faith. Who will be drawn to the Saviour of grumbling Christians? Contentment is a lesson which, like Paul, we need to learn.

There are many things which should make us contented. God's sovereignty, for example, the way in which he wisely and mercifully orders all things for our good. God's blessings should produce contentment in us. We should be contented because of his great and precious promises, both for this life and for that which is to come. But we should also be contented quite simply because we are not going to hell. John Wesley once wrote in his diary, 'At about eleven o'clock it came into my mind that this was the very day in which forty years ago I was taken out of the flames. The voice of praise and thanksgiving went up on high and great was our rejoicing before the Lord.' The remembrance of his deliverance from hell made Wesley happy.

One of the best cures for self-pity is to look at someone who is much worse off than ourselves. During a period of minor illness some time ago, when I tended to feel a bit sorry for myself, I would occasionally look down from my pulpit on a Sabbath morning at a member of the congregation. She was a gracious Christian, confined to a wheelchair by crippling disease. Her face was serene, steadfast in suffering, and my self-pity melted away in the warmth of her courage.

But we are all in that position, for we are surrounded by multitudes who are infinitely, eternally worse off than we are, millions on their way to hell. We are not, by Christ's grace, destined for damnation and yet we dare to complain! When next you think that life is treating you roughly and that God could have arranged your circumstances more lovingly, take a look into the pit of hell and remember, 'I was going there, but now I am not. Instead, I am on my way to heaven, for God has saved me. What are all the

---

[1] Cited in Blanchard, *Whatever Happened to Hell?*, p. 287.

disappointments, pains and sorrows of this life? They are nothing in comparison with what I deserve, nothing compared with what I will inherit'. This is what the Psalmist did: 'I will praise You, O Lord my God, with all my heart, and I will glorify Your name for evermore. For great is Your mercy toward me, and You have delivered my soul from the depths of Sheol' (*Psa.* 86:12–13).

The doctrine of hell should make believers supremely contented, grateful to God in every circumstance of life.

Seriousness
Thirdly, the reality of hell should be reflected in a pervasive seriousness in our thinking and behaviour.

It seems that, for some evangelicals today, the cardinal mistake is gloom and their greatest fear is of appearing morbid. The predominant emphasis of much church publicity is that Christianity is lots of fun. In many churches the prevailing atmosphere is one of compulsory, rather frantic joviality. Whoever presides over the meetings will have a neat line in humour, proving himself an expert in 'warming up' the audience (no longer a congregation). Christian testimonies are unremittingly upbeat and are punctuated by roars of laughter. Those who welcome us at the door keep smiling so broadly that we are tempted to conclude that they have just had their teeth capped or are practising ventriloquism. (Is a permanent grin generally considered an indicator of rationality?) But such, they seem to believe, is an integral part of Christian witness.

Yet the Lord Jesus Christ is not pictured in the gospels as a jolly, chuckling figure. He himself said, 'Blessed are those who mourn' (*Matt.* 5:4). Isaiah described him as 'a man of sorrows and acquainted with grief' (*Isa.* 53:3). So should we imitate our contemporaries or our Master? Should we be more serious than jovial?

We must be, as long as there is a hell awaiting new occupants. How can we go through life giggling while millions around us are on their way to damnation? If a plague were raging, with dead bodies lying everywhere, what would you think of people who skipped light-heartedly through the corpses, laughing because they had found a cure for themselves? The psalmist grieved over the sin around him, as he testified to God that: 'Rivers of water run down from my eyes, because men do not keep Your law' (*Psa.* 119:136).

This does not mean that believers are to be morose. We experience a joy unspeakable and full of glory. We rejoice evermore. We have fun, we laugh, we play, we enjoy to the full the good gifts of God. But there is a difference between happiness and frivolity. An awareness of hell should produce in us an underlying seriousness, a gravity, a realism among the lost and dying.

Particularly is this the case when we are dealing with such fearful truths as death, judgment and eternal condemnation. There is a place for humour, but it is not here. Here, above all, the Christian buffoon is an abomination. And yet these realities are treated facetiously and sometimes by surprising people. A celebrated minister, recently asked if everyone in his church was converted, smilingly replied, 'Well, I certainly wouldn't like to be handcuffed to some of my church members when they die'. His listeners burst out laughing. But is that amusing? Would you make that comment about a close friend or one of your children who was unconverted? Is there not a startling lack of sensitivity about any Christian community which can laugh at hell?

Our flaws and foibles can be amusing. Life has a funny side and human beings are often laughable, not least the writer of these pages. But sin and its results are never amusing. J. P. Struthers, a much-loved Scottish minister in the early years of the last century, was walking one evening along the streets of Greenock, the town in which he lived and ministered. In the distance a drunk man was staggering in circles, shouting and singing, making a fool of himself and surrounded by a group of laughing locals. As Struthers drew near, he saw several of his own members in the crowd. Quietly, the minister stepped among them, looked round and said, 'For many walk, of whom I have told you often, and now tell you even weeping – weeping – that they are the enemies of the cross of Christ' (*Phil.* 3:18). Shamefaced and silent, the people moved away.

Unconverted people may call us gloomy. They may consider our meetings old-fashioned and dull, without the sparkle of the polished ecclesiastical comedians. That cannot be helped. But when they are in trouble, in a real crisis, will they turn to the clowns? Will they look for someone to tell them little stories and make them laugh? Time and again we find that people in need are drawn instinctively to those who are serious, in earnest, in touch with real life. They sense a sterling character, an ability to help on a profound level. In the long run, the jester has less impact than the man or woman with tears of compassion. Those who once mocked us may come to discover that 'it is better to hear the rebuke of the wise than for a man to hear the song of fools' (*Eccles.* 7:5).

Let us be serious, let us be thoughtful, as we live in a world where so many of our fellow creatures are perishing.

APPRECIATION OF CHRIST

Fourthly, the doctrine of hell should lead us to appreciate more than we do the love and merits of the Lord Jesus Christ. Peter says that though we have not seen him we love him (*1 Pet.* 1:8). That is true, and we long to love him more deeply. How can we? By recognizing a principle which he himself stated: 'To whom little is forgiven, the same loves little' (*Luke* 7:47), implying that to whom much is forgiven, the same loves much.

How much have we been forgiven? From how much have we been spared? What did it cost to save us? We know that Christ came to earth for us, and that he lived, suffered and died on our behalf. All of this is wonderful beyond comparison. But it is not until we gaze into hell that we really appreciate the love of our Saviour.

We have tried in a limited and inadequate way to imagine what hell must be like and have found the prospect appalling. But the Lord Jesus does not need to use his imagination, for he has experienced it for himself. He knows what separation from God means. He has endured the agonizing pains, he has drunk to the dregs the cup of divine wrath. The Lord has laid on him the iniquity of us all. God did not spare his own Son, but visited on him all the fury of holy judgment. Christ accepted my damnation, suffered my hell. He took that horror upon himself because he loved me. Should I not love him?

More than this, hell gives us a new insight into the value of Christ's death. We have glimpsed something of how terrible the punishment will be for each condemned sinner. An eternity in hell will not begin to exhaust God's anger. Yet it is all deserved. Sin against an infinite God demands an infinite and everlasting penalty. But the death of the Lord Jesus Christ was sufficient to atone fully for all the sins of all his people. On the hill of Calvary he made full payment for the guilt of the elect. How infinitely worthy that death must be! We can hardly begin even to conceive of it. How great a being he must be, how unimaginably precious his self-offering, that he could end his sufferings with the triumphant cry, 'It is finished' (*John* 19:30). His blood is able to cleanse us from all sin. God the Father has pronounced himself satisfied with the atonement made on that afternoon for such a massive weight of evil. This is stupendous! Well might Paul say, 'God forbid that I should boast except in the cross of our Lord Jesus Christ' (*Gal.* 6:14).

Hell brings us to our knees, moving us to wonder and gratitude. Hell inspires us with a new adoration for him who loved us and gave himself for us. His death destroyed and cancelled hell for us. That is what he is worth; that is who he is.

When we believe in Jesus we are linked with a being of unimaginable power, glory and grace. It is not a small thing to trust in Christ. It is not a trivial matter when he invites us to 'Come to Me' (*Matt.* 11:28). He is the infinite God, whose love fills and transcends our comprehension. This mighty Saviour, in his majesty and kindness, summons us to the salvation which he has provided for us at the cost of his own death-agony. If we do not come to love more intensely the Lord who saves us from hell by having experienced it for himself, then we have studied this topic in vain.

ZEAL FOR EVANGELISM

One of the most obvious results of a consideration of hell should be a renewed zeal for evangelism. The very content of the doctrine demands it. People all around us are heading for this terrible place. Only the gospel will point them to the way of salvation. We have been entrusted with that message and have been delivered from hell ourselves only because someone communicated it to us. Our responsibility is immense and inescapable. We owe it to our fellow-men to tell them about the Saviour. Evangelism is a prime Christian duty and we have reason to thank God for countless efforts being made all over the globe to bring people to Christ.

But how do we measure up ourselves? Are we as faithful as we should be in communicating the gospel? Or is this, like prayer, a matter about which we feel the stab of an uneasy conscience? Robert L. Dabney has an interesting comment in his discussion of the heresy of Universalism, the belief that all will eventually be saved. For he claims that, apart from philosophical and theological arguments, 'the chief practical argument in favour of Universalism is doubtless the sinful callousness of Christians towards this tremendous destiny of their sinful fellow creatures. Can we contemplate the exposure of our friends, neighbours, and children to a fate so terrible, and feel so little sensibility and make efforts so few and weak for their deliverance? How can our unbelieving friends be made to credit the sincerity of our convictions? Here is the best argument of Satan for their scepticism.'[1]

Dabney's assessment is both penetrating and troubling. If we do not evangelize, we are in effect saying that we do not really believe in hell. If we meant what we profess to believe, we would surely do more for the salvation of the lost. He goes on to say that 'the best refutation of this heresy is the exhibition by God's people of a holy, tender, humble yet burning zeal to pluck men as brands from the burning.'[2]

How many of us were more in earnest for witnessing in the days when we were young Christians? In the dawn of our new commitment we had a kind of innocent simplicity. We longed for the salvation of our friends. We expected them to come to faith. A key part of our daily devotions was prayer for opportunities to tell of Christ. We know more now, of course, or so we think. That far-off enthusiasm can seem superficial, even embarrassing. But perhaps we should be more ashamed of our present than our past. Our zeal has grown cold and we have left our first love.

The devil is clever enough to turn our strengths into weaknesses. Healthy Christians love the Word of God. It is sheer delight to us, individually and corporately, to explore the profound revelation in Scripture of his wisdom and grace. We feel that we have only begun to examine this treasure, that we are still at the fringes of what the Lord has told us. We have, at our best, a passionate, God-implanted longing to learn more and more of his truth. But the danger is for us to become so absorbed in study, so devoted to developing our doctrinal understanding, that we forget the ruined, dying masses all around us.

As Christians, we have many responsibilities. Some of our churches need to be re-structured along more biblical lines. The people of God

---

[1] *Systematic Theology,* pp. 861–2.
[2] *Ibid.*

need training and nurture. Many issues in society call for Christian input. But to neglect evangelism is failure on a massive scale.

And it is in this area that other believers can challenge us by their overwhelming zeal, their passion for the lost, their commitment to prayer and to bold, imaginative activity. Their theology may be defective, their evangelism unbalanced, their methodology suspect and none of these can be defended. But their enthusiasm is commendable, their zeal a rebuke and a stimulus to us. God who, as the Puritans loved to say, 'can draw a straight line with a crooked stick', blesses their compassionate, believing witness and uses them to bring many to faith.

I am not arguing for unreflecting activism, for carelessness or superficiality. But are we in a position to criticize those who are doing imperfectly what we may not be doing at all? Where is our zeal? Where is our explosive commitment, driving us out 'into the streets and lanes of the city' for 'the poor and the maimed and the lame and the blind' – out into 'the highways and hedges' to 'compel them to come in'(*Luke* 14:21, 23)? Perhaps the voice of God should come as a rebuke to those who like to criticize from the sidelines, 'Hypocrite! Why do you look at the speck in your brother's eye, but do not consider the plank in your own eye? It is six months since you have spoken to another human being about faith in Christ, and yet you dare to find fault with that brother or sister who, in your opinion, is doing it improperly?'

The doctrine of hell should motivate us to speak out. We need to repent of our apathy and hardness of heart. We should gaze into hell until we can almost feel the pain which awaits the unconverted. John Blanchard tells of an occasion when Francis Schaeffer was visibly moved by the thought of hell. In his chalet in Switzerland he was explaining Scripture to a group of young people. Intelligent and inquisitive, they admired their teacher's unique ability to relate God's Word to contemporary culture. Various topics were covered, until eventually a young man asked, 'Dr Schaeffer, what about those who have never heard the gospel?' They waited expectantly for the incisively brilliant answer. But Schaeffer did not speak. Instead, he bowed his head and wept.[1]

---

[1] See *Whatever Happened to Hell?*, pp. 114–5,

Hudson Taylor, the great missionary leader of the late nineteenth century, made the same point in a different way. Speaking on furlough to a large audience, he told about a man falling into a river in China. As he struggled in the water, those on the bank simply stood and watched. No-one moved to help him and the wretched man drowned. Taylor's hearers gasped in horror at such indifference, but he was ready with his challenge. 'Men and women of England, millions are perishing at this moment. What are you doing to rescue them?'

Is there someone to whom you should speak – a neighbour, a colleague, a member of your family? Each of us should have a specific burden of concern for at least one person and should determine to do all we can for their salvation. We should love them, cultivate their friendship, pray for them daily, speak of our Saviour as opportunity permits, invite them to hear the preaching of the Word. If you have not been doing that recently, will you begin now? For whom will you pray before you sleep tonight?

HUMBLE ACCEPTANCE OF GOD'S SOVEREIGN PURPOSES

Hell should produce in us, lastly, a humble acceptance of God's sovereign purposes, with reference both to our present responsibility and to the existence of hell itself.

If we are not deeply concerned for the unconverted, there is something seriously wrong with us. Paul wrote, 'I have great sorrow and continual grief in my heart. for my brethren . . . according to the flesh' (*Rom.* 9:2-3). He was burdened for his fellow-Jews and the prospect of their damnation was an agony to him. We should experience a similar grief. We should be moved for the lost, passionately committed to spreading the gospel by every means in our power. Nothing, as we have seen, should be allowed to blunt that sense of responsibility.

But does our duty to evangelize over-ride everything else in life? Are we justified in concluding that, in view of the existence of hell, we should abandon all other activities and give ourselves to full-time evangelism? Would we be right in assuming that the only worthwhile occupation for believers is proclaiming the gospel to those on their way to judgment?

Not if we understand the balanced teaching of Scripture. God calls few of his people to such focused ministry. Everyday life on earth must continue. Humans are to sow and reap, to marry and reproduce, to exercise dominion over creation in their various callings. His will for you is to live out your faith in the situation in which he has placed you, nurturing a family perhaps, doing your daily work in a godly way, using your gifts to serve in church and community.

Our responsibility for others, though real, is limited. Ultimately, if people go to hell, they have no-one to blame but themselves, for God says, 'The soul who sins shall die. The son shall not bear the guilt of the father, nor the father bear the guilt of the son. The righteousness of the righteous shall be upon himself, and the wickedness of the wicked shall be upon himself' (*Ezek*. 18:20). If we fail to tell our friends about Christ we will be held partly accountable for their damnation, but the final responsibility rests with the individual concerned.

Do not accept more responsibility than that which God puts on you. If you do, it will break you. I have seen sensitive pastors broken. In their very conscientiousness they took upon themselves a burden too heavy for any mortal to bear. God is the Lord. We need not be afraid that, if we do not immediately evangelize everyone we know, they will drop into hell by mistake. Christ will save every one of his chosen people. He reassures us that 'All that the Father gives Me will come to Me', and that 'Those whom You gave Me I have kept; and none of them is lost' (*John* 6:37; 17:12).

Paradoxical as it may seem, we need to relax, to rest in God's sovereignty. Some of you may be burdened for the salvation of your children. You have prayed for them, taught them the Scriptures and urged them to believe, all with no visible results so far. Your deep concern for them will continue – and it should. God forbid that you ever become apathetic or indifferent. You may have regrets over past mistakes and inconsistencies. For these you will seek and obtain forgiveness. But you must exercise faith in the Lord. I remember talking in Edinburgh with a man of sixty-four who had just become a Christian. His godly parents had died years earlier, heartbroken over their wayward son who had repudiated their faith and their example. But the time came when he was converted and he told me that he attributed his conversion, under God, to the prayers of his father and mother. They had died without seeing him a believer, but their prayers for him had not been in vain. This may not always happen, of course, but we must trust the Almighty. The gift of salvation is not in our hands, it is not within our power to confer it and we have to commit even our nearest and dearest to him. We cannot bear responsibility for the souls of others. We may have to live with the anguish of seeing them rejecting Christ, but we must not let ourselves be shattered by their unbelief. God makes no mistakes. Our duty is to trust in him.

Finally, we have to accept humbly God's sovereign purpose in creating hell. To think of it is dreadful and we cannot help feeling deeply for our fellow human beings who are lost. It is right that we should. We are commanded to love our enemies as well as our neighbour, for they too are created in God's image. For all we know, they may be much more than that. The most evil person you have ever met may be one of the elect. He may seem to be a devil incarnate, a Saul of Tarsus, and yet he may prove to be one of those whom God chose in eternity, and whom he plans to redeem. We must grieve intensely over the damnation of even a single individual.

Yet our natural compassion can very easily slip over into a dislike of the doctrine of hell itself. John Stott has written about everlasting punishment that, 'Emotionally I find the concept intolerable and do not understand how people can live with it without either cauterizing their emotions or cracking under the strain.'[1] This is an increasingly common view, not only about eternal punishment but in regard to the whole idea of hell. People are saying, in other words, that they would prefer it if there were no such place.

Such feelings are understandable. But are they right? Should we see hell as a distasteful, embarrassing reality, one that we really wish did not exist? The problem with this view is that Scripture shows us the glorified saints praising God for his judgment upon sin and worshipping him for overthrowing wickedness: 'We give You thanks, O Lord God Almighty, because You have taken Your great power and reigned. You are righteous, O Lord, because You

---

[1] Edwards and Stott, *Essentials, A Liberal-Evangelical Dialogue*, p. 314.

have judged these things. For they have shed the blood of saints and prophets, and You have given them blood to drink. For it is their just due' (*Rev*. 11:17; 16:5–6).

It appears that the saints in heaven praise God for hell. Should we praise him for it now? Let us be careful here. We can certainly give thanks to God that there is a hell for sin. We can say, 'Thank you Lord, that you have prepared fire for the devil and his angels. I am glad that he will be there for ever and ever. I rejoice that wickedness will be condemned and I praise you Lord for that place of punishment.'

But can we go further? Can we thank God that there is a hell for wicked people? I would be very reluctant to do it. As I look into my own heart, I see too much sin, too much self-centredness, malice and pride. It is only because of the Saviour's grace that I am not in hell myself. I simply cannot look at another sinner and thank God for the punishment which awaits him or her. There is surely an un-Christlike bitterness of soul in someone who can feel anything but anguish at the eventual fate of the lost.

When we are in heaven, however, we will praise God for all that he accomplishes by means of hell. For we will be purged of sin, our motives will be entirely holy and we will be filled with the mind of Christ. God's just and righteous judgment will be revealed. All the inequities of this life will be swept away. All the apparent unfairnesses and mysteries of time will be solved. Everything will be made right. The Lord's majesty will shine forth and all those who have arrogantly raised themselves up against him will be humbled and cast down. God will be glorified in hell, and if the glory of God means more to us than anything else, can we be sorry that hell exists? We cannot; and in heaven we will be transformed, able to worship God for all that he has done, including hell.

What an awesome mystery! In Jonathan Edwards' carefully chosen words, 'It becomes the saints fully and perfectly to consent to what God doth, without any reluctance or opposition of spirit; yea, it becomes them to rejoice in everything that God sees meet to be done.'[1]

---

[1] 'The end of the wicked contemplated by the righteous', *Works*, Vol. 2, Edinburgh: Banner of Truth, 1974, p. 210.

We dare not yet aspire to that. But we will. We cannot now grasp how, in the purposes of God, he is glorified through hell. But we will. This truth, like all others, brings us to our knees and moves us to worship.

5
Heaven Matters

WHILE ANY THOUGHT OF HELL IS ANATHEMA to most people, the doctrine of heaven is probably the most popular of all Christian teachings. A poll, taken in the United States in 1990, reported that seventy-eight per cent of those questioned claimed to believe in heaven. In a supposedly materialistic age, there is a widespread fascination with life after death. Well over one hundred books about angels are currently in print. Titles such as *Embraced by the Light* and *Caught up into Paradise* top the best seller lists. Television programmes dealing with the supernatural command large audiences. Heaven is a fashionable subject.

This is not just a recent development, for belief in an after-life is common to all humanity. God, we are told, 'has put eternity in their hearts' (*Eccles.* 3:11) and human beings seem to know instinctively that there is another life beyond this one. In the pyramids of Egypt the embalmed bodies had maps beside them as a guide for the future world. The Greeks and the Romans believed in a spirit world into which the dead would enter. Native Americans buried bows and arrows in their tribal graves for use in the happy hunting ground. Today we hear of women asking for their make-up bag and favourite magazines to be buried with them. Belief in a life to come is a constant element in human culture.

And yet there is a paradox in all of this. Many people say they believe in heaven, but their interest in it is superficial. This belief does not seem to make any difference to the way they live. It has no practical impact upon their behaviour. To all intents and purposes they ignore that future which they hope to experience and enjoy.

More perplexingly still, we find within Christianity itself less interest in heaven than at almost any time in history. Few valuable modern books have been written on this topic. One of the great text books of Reformed theology is Louis Berkhof's *Systematic Theology*, yet Berkhof, strangely, devotes only one of his 784 pages to the subject of heaven. It is not often preached about. Christians, when they meet together, rarely discuss the life to come and the prospect of glory. We may be surprised that unbelievers are so unaffected by thoughts of the heaven in which they say they believe. Yet it is surely more baffling that we, who through faith in Christ have good reason to anticipate going to heaven and being there for ever, devote to it so little time or attention.

Why is the doctrine of heaven neglected? And why is such neglect so harmful?

WHY IS HEAVEN NEGLECTED?

One obvious reason why many of us do not reflect on heaven nearly as much as we should is that we are too preoccupied with this present world. We are surrounded by what we can see and hear, touch, taste and smell. If I take a coin in my hand and hold it close to my eye, it will block out the sun and I will see nothing but that small shiny coin. Now the sun is bigger than a coin, but because the coin is close it blocks from my sight something incomparably greater. The daily realities of life may be neither big nor, ultimately, important, but they are close to us, they impinge upon us. And the danger is that the very closeness of this world blocks out the infinitely vaster prospect of the glorious world which is to come.

Another reason for neglecting heaven is that, at least in the western world, we are too comfortable. For the most part we are comparatively rich, reasonably healthy, tolerably happy. Life is sweet and, without realizing it, we are drugged by well-being and prosperity. Tragedy stabs us awake and makes us suddenly and poignantly aware of heaven and hell. A loved one becomes seriously ill and we find in an instant that heaven is no longer theoretical or far away. It is very real and we long to find out more about it. But for much of the time we are content as we are. Other generations of believers had more of the pilgrim spirit. 'This world is not my home', they sang, 'I'm simply passing through'. They described themselves as 'pilgrims through this barren land'. But our world is a rich world, a pleasant world, and we have put down roots. We have traded 'the sweet by and by' for the prosperous here and now. This is an era of instant gratification and there is so much to enjoy in the present. Society offers us a dazzling range of experiences, from the new technologies of interactive entertainment to ever more exotic foreign holidays. The very comfort of this world makes heaven less inviting.

Or we can neglect heaven because we see it as nothing more than the inevitable next stage in our existence. This is certainly how unbelievers think. But many professing Christians have a similar view. We believe in heaven, it is something that will happen in the future, and when it does we will no doubt enjoy it. But in the meantime, why waste time wondering about it? How will daydreams help us? Heaven will come when it comes. Time enough to think about it then.

We may neglect heaven because it simply doesn't appeal to us. As a child I had no desire to go to heaven, for it seemed to me a boring place. My vision was of a church service which went on and on for millions of years, while I had to sit in a spotlessly white suit on a marble seat, not allowed to move throughout all eternity. Such a view of everlasting life was of limited appeal to a small boy! Of course, when the subject came up at home I feigned a decent enthusiasm, but it was largely synthetic. I didn't like the sound of heaven and was in no hurry to go there.

We may have outgrown such childish misconceptions, but we can still be curiously apathetic about heaven, clumsy at understanding or communicating its beauty. Literary critics have commented on the difference between John Milton's two great poems *Paradise Lost* and *Paradise Regained*. *Paradise Lost* is a superior work, more vivid, colourful and gripping, while *Paradise Regained* is at times bland and rather lifeless. Milton seemed to find it easier to write about hell than about heaven. In some ways, heaven is not attractive to us. There is truth as well as tragic humour in the story of a woman who was asked about a friend who had died and who answered rather impatiently, 'Well I suppose she is enjoying eternal bliss, but I don't want to talk about such an unpleasant subject'!

Christians are sometimes brainwashed into neglecting heaven. We can be too eager to please those outside the church, anxiously asking them what they expect from us and assuring them that we will try to provide it. And the world claims to want what is obviously relevant. 'If you have nothing practical to teach us', they say, 'we don't want to listen to you. We need help for the here and now, for today and tomorrow. What concrete benefit will your message bring me now? How can I put it to use? Don't talk to me about 'pie-in-the-sky'. I'm not interested in an airy-fairy future world.' And too often in the church we have capitulated to that thinking and have neglected the glory to come. One of the most damaging slogans of Satan has been the criticism that Christians are too heavenly-minded to be of any earthly use. We want to be useful on earth, of course, and we think that the answer is to be less heavenly-minded. On the contrary, as we shall see, it is only those who are heavenly-minded who are ultimately of much earthly use at all.

This accusation has been a master-stroke of the devil. His influence is behind much of our neglect of heaven. For it is in his interest to cause us to neglect it, to blind our minds to this glorious possibility, and to focus our attention short-sightedly on the immediate present.

Finally, we may neglect heaven because it is a reality too awesome for our limited minds to grasp. It is too magnificent for us, too transcendent, too glorious. Our little brains cannot manage heaven. As Paul writes, 'Eye has not seen, nor ear heard, nor have entered into the heart of man the things which God has prepared for those who love him' (*1 Cor.* 2:9, quoting *Isa.* 64:4). It is simply beyond our comprehension.

For these reasons, among others, heaven is a neglected doctrine.

WHY DOES THE SUBJECT OF HEAVEN MATTER?

But does it matter that we do not think of heaven as often as we should? It matters profoundly.

It matters first because many people who take it for granted that they are going to heaven are not. There is no evidence in their lives that they are joined to Christ. They are nurturing a false hope. We hear the flippant comments that are passed when famous men or women die. Someone says that they are looking down from above, pleasantly surprised by the large and impressive attendance at their funeral. We hear about how golfers are enjoying playing golf and fishermen are getting huge catches in heaven. They may have shown little interest in the things of God, they may never have professed faith in the Saviour, but it is taken for granted that heaven is where they now find themselves. To suggest otherwise is to be branded a ghoulish bigot. We talk to people who assume that they are going to heaven and yet they have no good reason for their careless assumption. They are facing a most appalling shock. Their neglect of heaven is lethal.

It matters again because many popular ideas about the life to come are grotesquely inaccurate. Most of the current best-sellers about heaven are a toxic mixture of misquoted Bible verses, New Age philosophy, Mormonism, the occult, empty sentiment and superstition. This hodge-podge of confusion and falsehood is deluding people, not all of whom, sadly, are outside the church. Their minds are being poisoned. 'Nature abhors a vacuum', and if truth is not taught, error will replace it.

Our neglect matters because, as Christians, we are throwing away one of our most powerful evangelistic weapons. God offers to sinful, miserable human beings an eternity of unimaginable happiness. What a stupendously glorious possibility! But the Church is not shouting this message from the housetops. The French novelist Victor Hugo was inaccurate in his theology but accurate in his sentiment when he wrote, 'I am the tadpole of an archangel.' He believed, in other words, that human beings are destined for a greater and better future. Yet the evangelical church today is concentrating on helping people to become better tadpoles. Go to any Christian bookstore and see what so many of the books are about: not about God or heaven, not about the world to come. They are about becoming better tadpoles, making limited, temporary improvements in our life here and now. Is this all the Church can offer – 'Christ can give you peace of mind; Christ can give you a better marriage; Christ can teach you how to train your children'? People can find painkillers and parenting classes that will promise as much. What about the fact that Jesus Christ can bring you to glory forever? We are not telling people that, and then we are surprised when they are not interested in the gospel. We are not using one of the most wonderful truths which God has placed in his Word. Of course it is harmful to neglect heaven.

But, lastly, it matters for our own sakes – for our spiritual growth and our effectiveness in service. By neglecting what the Bible says about heaven we leave ourselves as believers much poorer, weaker and more troubled than we need be. Most of the teaching about heaven in Scripture is not for evangelism but for pastoring the people of God. He explains heaven in his Word primarily for his own children's sake, to help and comfort us, to encourage and strengthen us, to make us more holy, to fill us with joy. The doctrine of heaven is revealed to shine light on your life and mine here and now, to enable us to be better people today and tomorrow. We cheat ourselves if we do not make use of this wonderful teaching. It is an immense blessing to know much more about heaven. And we can know. We do not need to be left in the dark.

Did you spot the misleading partial quotation several paragraphs ago? Mentioning the transcendence of heaven, I quoted 1 Corinthians 2:9: 'Eye has not seen, nor ear heard, neither have entered into the heart of man the things that God has prepared for those who love him.' But there I stopped – inexcusably! For what does the next verse say? 'But God has revealed them to us through his Spirit'. How often this passage is misused! Heaven is too great to understand, say the writers and the preachers, and they quote verse nine. But that is not at all what Paul is saying. Quite the reverse. He is telling us that, while heaven is too great for unconverted people to understand, too magnificent to be grasped by unaided human reason, God has revealed these things to us by his Spirit. With his Word in our hands we can know about heaven. He means us to learn about it and to neglect it no longer.

Where should we begin? By considering the context within which our whole understanding of heaven must be placed.

6

Created for God's Glory

H EAVEN IS A FASCINATING SUBJECT and there is much about it that we
long to discover. But it is vital to begin in the right way, for if we
are wrongly orientated at the start we will never recover. It would be
a mistake to be impatient and rush into our study without pausing to
take our bearings. We can find an appropriate starting point in words
of God recorded in Isaiah 43:7: 'Created for My glory'. He originally
applied this phrase to his own people, to 'everyone who is called by
My name'. But it is true in a more general sense of all that God
creates and all that he does. And it is particularly true of heaven.
Heaven is created for God's glory. This is the foundation upon which
all our thinking must rest.

GOD'S GLORY DISPLAYED
The very first words of the Bible are: 'In the beginning God created
the heavens and the earth'. Have you ever asked yourself why God
chose to create the heavens and the earth? He did not need to, for he
did not need anyone or anything. As Father, Son and Spirit he has
always been perfectly self-sufficient. He always will be. He is the God
with no needs (*Acts* 17:25). But he must have had a purpose in
creating the heavens and the earth. What was it? He did not act on a

whim; he did not do it because he was bored or needed something to occupy his time.

The most satisfying answer I have found is in the discourse by Jonathan Edwards entitled 'The End for which God Created the World'.[1] With typical thoroughness, Edwards sets himself to address that question. His answer is: 'That there might be a glorious and abundant emanation of his infinite fulness of good *ad extra*, or without himself.' He continues: 'This disposition to communicate himself, or diffuse his own fulness was what moved him to create the world'. God had a 'disposition to communicate himself', to spread abroad his own fullness. His purpose was for his goodness to over-spill his own Being, as it were. He chose to create the heavens and the earth so that his glory could come pouring out from himself in abundance. He brought a physical reality into existence in order that it might experience his glory and be filled with it and reflect it – every atom, every second, every part and moment of creation. He made human beings in his own image to reflect his glory, and he placed them in a perfect environment which also reflected it. 'God saw everything that He had made, and indeed it was very good' (*Gen.* 1:31). The heavens and the earth displayed his glory.

THE 'HEAVENS'

When we read that God created the heavens and the earth, what does the word 'heavens' mean? The original meaning of the Hebrew and Greek terms is uncertain, but they came to describe that which is over-arching, lofty, the upper regions. Heaven is the sky, that which is high and raised up. In the Bible it is used of three separate and yet inter-connected entities.

It refers first of all to the atmosphere: the air above us which envelops this planet. 'The rain comes down and the snow from heaven' (*Isa.* 55:10). 'The dew of heaven' (*Dan.* 4:15) is so called because it comes down from the sky, from the air. We also read of the 'birds of the heavens' (*Jer.* 4:25). The frost, the wind, the clouds and the vapours, the thunder and the hail, all of these come from heaven. And we understand what that heaven is. It is the atmosphere, the air above us.

[1] *Works, Vol. 2*, pp. 94–121.
[2] *Ibid.*, p. 100.

Secondly there is what we now call 'space'. The Bible sometimes describes this region as the 'firmament' or the 'expanse'. In Genesis 1:14, God calls for lights in 'the firmament of the heavens (NIV: 'the expanse of the sky') to divide the day from the night'. What does he mean when he says this? He is referring to the location of the sun, the moon and the stars. The planets and the galaxies are in these heavens. So the word 'heaven' in Scripture refers to the atmosphere and also to space, the planetary heavens.

Of course, in thinking about the biblical doctrine of heaven, we will not be spending time on either the atmosphere or space. But we should reflect for a moment before moving on to our real subject, because it is not an accident of vocabulary that these entities are called by the same word as the dwelling place of God. This does not happen because of a shortage of words in Hebrew or Greek. No, we are meant to see a relationship between them. The sky and space speak to us of the true heaven. They bear witness to the glory and power of the Creator. 'The heavens declare the glory of God', the psalmist says, 'and the firmament shows his handiwork' (*Psa.* 19:1). God's rainbow in the heavens assures us that his covenant promise is certain (*Gen.* 9:13–17). The stars remind us of God's promise of innumerable descendants to his chosen servant, for he said to Abraham, 'Count the stars if you are able. So shall your descendants be' (*Gen.* 15:5).

These heavens also speak to us of our limitations and our littleness. The Psalmist exclaims, 'When I consider Your heavens, the work of Your fingers . . . What is man that You are mindful of him?' (*Psa.* 8:3–4). Astronomers tell us that the nearest star to our solar system is seventeen million million miles away. Yet God 'counts the number of the stars' and 'calls them all by name' (*Psa.* 147:4). How awesome and majestic he must be! In the words of the prophet Isaiah, 'Who has measured the waters in the hollow of his hand, measured heaven with a span, and calculated the dust of the earth in a measure?' (*Isa.* 40:12).

We live in cities with artificial lighting and we rarely have a clear view of the stars in the night sky. Experts tell us what the weather is going to be like and we think of snow and rain not as coming down from above but in terms of 'depressions' and 'cold fronts'. We do not often look up to the heavens or think of them. But it is no mere coincidence of language that in the Bible the atmosphere and space are called the heavens. We are meant to turn our eyes upwards and admire the glory, majesty and power of the Creator. We should note his goodness to us in giving us fruitful rain from heaven (*Acts* 14:17). These heavens do speak to us of 'the' heaven and of the God of heaven. They are the Lord's witness to all humanity.

'HEAVEN ITSELF'

But we come now to 'heaven itself'. That is a scriptural phrase. We are told that Christ has entered 'into heaven itself' (*Heb.* 9:24): not the atmosphere, not space, but heaven itself. The Old Testament calls this place the 'highest heaven', 'the heaven of heavens' (2 *Chron.* 2:6). Paul, perhaps thinking of the atmosphere as the first heaven and space as the second, refers to it as the 'third heaven' (2 *Cor.* 12:2). We are not told where this heaven, the highest heaven, is, but the Bible describes it as the dwelling place of God. 'Look down from heaven . . . your habitation, holy and glorious', prays the prophet (*Isa.* 63:15). King David looks forward to dwelling 'in the house of the Lord forever' (*Psa.* 23:6). Heaven is God's home. We pray to 'Our Father in heaven'.

If you are philosophically minded, you may object to this idea. Surely God is present everywhere and cannot be limited by space or time. Yes, that is perfectly true. King Solomon says that heaven and the heaven of heavens cannot contain him (1 *Kings* 8:27). God cannot be restricted to any place, no matter how vast. So in what sense can we say that heaven is God's dwelling place? If God is present everywhere, how then is heaven his home?

Perhaps we have a clue in the word 'home'. Home is where we can be ourselves. If you want to know a person, you must see them at home. You will not learn so much about them at work, or out in society smartly dressed and on their best behaviour. But at home you see the person as he really is.

Although God is present everywhere in his power and wisdom, in his holiness and justice, heaven is his home. And when we say that, we mean that heaven is where God most clearly reveals himself and where we see him as he really is, in the fullness of his Being. John Owen puts it this way: 'The reason why God is said to be in heaven is, not because his essence is included in a certain place so called, but because of the more eminent manifestations of his glory there'.[1] Heaven is where God's magnificence is expressly revealed, his perfections shining in unimaginable splendour and beauty. Heaven is the place of God's glory.

That is why it is sometimes described in the Bible and in our everyday speech as 'glory'. Believers often say of friends who have died that they have 'gone to glory', meaning that they have gone to heaven. The psalmist says, 'You will guide me with Your counsel, and afterward receive me to glory' (*Psa*. 73:24). He is confident that God will receive him into heaven. We are told that Jesus brings many sons to glory (*Heb*. 2:10). Heaven is so intimately identified with glory that the two terms are almost interchangeable.

'Created for my glory.' Heaven is the arena of glory. This is why God created the heavens and the earth. It was a universe of stunning variety and richness, the man and the woman God's splendid image-bearers, the Lord walking with them in unbroken fellowship in the garden in the cool of the day. All reflected the excellencies of God. The glory of God shone forth. It was all very good.

GOD'S GLORY DIMINISHED

But this blessed state of affairs did not continue. The devil tempted Adam and Eve and they listened. They disobeyed God, they fell from their high position and the brightness of his image in them was tarnished. Human beings were separated from God. Death entered the world. God cursed the earth and its creatures. Paul tells us that 'the creation was subjected to futility', to 'the bondage of corruption' (*Rom*. 8:20–21). God's glory was diminished in the world which he had made.

What a tragedy! God created this earth and its inhabitants for his glory, but just a few chapters later in Genesis we read that 'the wickedness of man was great in the earth and that every intent of the thoughts of his heart was only evil continually . . . The earth also was corrupt before God, and the earth was filled with violence' (*Gen*. 6:5,11). These are heart-breaking words. A tidal wave of sin and misery is engulfing creation. But the most terrible tragedy of the Fall is not what it did to us or to the earth, but what it did to the handiwork of God, the havoc it wreaked in the theatre of God's glory.

[1]*Works, Vol. 12,* London: Banner of Truth, 1966, p. 90.

Look at the world in which we live. What is it like? Look at the people in high places, the powerful, the opinion-formers, the élite. What sort of people are they? Are many of them noble or pure, truthful or loving? Consider the increasing corruption of our society. Is it not all too obvious that humans 'fall short of the glory of God' (*Rom.* 3:23)? Look at our planet with its contaminated air and water, its floods and whirlwinds, its wars, disease and famine.

It seems as if Satan has won a great victory by defacing what God has created, by making contemptible the revelation of God's glory. The glory is still visible, of course. We can see flashes of it here and there and from time to time. Yet how pitifully little by comparison!

God's glory was displayed; God's glory has been diminished; but God's glory is also restored.

GOD'S GLORY RESTORED

Here, praise God, is where heaven comes in. In spite of all the sin and tragedy there is one untouched, uncontaminated, created realm where God's glory still shines in transcendent beauty – and that is heaven. Satan has been banished from heaven. In that joyful place the holy angels worship and serve the Lord in all his majesty and splendour. In heaven God's glory has always shone. In heaven it keeps on shining.

It is from that bright region that the crushing counter-attack comes. Heaven is the place from which God's glory returns to earth to make earth and its people glorious. The story of the Bible is the story of heaven coming back to this world, taking it over and filling it once again. It is about the revelation and restoration of God's glory, and that in a far richer and more wonderful way in Christ than ever was seen in Eden or in Adam.

So God begins to work in history. Everything that he does is for one reason – for his glory. That is God's purpose and passion. He elects a people in eternity. Why? For his glory. He chooses Israel for his glory. He delivers them from Egypt for his glory. He restores them after exile for his glory. As you read the Old Testament, say to yourself, 'The glory is coming, the glory is coming!' On every page, in every era of Israel's history, the glory is coming.

Then at last God sends his Son. When Christ is born the heavens are opened and a multitude of the heavenly host is praising God.

Their theme? 'Glory to God in the highest and on earth peace, good will toward men' (*Luke* 2:14). John says that God's glory was visible in Jesus of Nazareth, 'the glory as of the only begotten of the Father' (*John* 1:14). Jesus smashed the devil, glory's enemy. He lived a perfect life and died an atoning death to pay for the sins of his people. As he came towards the cross, he summed up his life and work in these words: 'I have glorified You on the earth. I have finished the work which You have given me to do' (*John* 17:4). After his death and resurrection he returned to the glory from which he had come.

And the glory of heaven, which Christ possessed and revealed, and for which he lived and died, is transmitted to others. At the very moment in which people believe in him, it can be said that they enter heaven. Believers receive and enter glory. We pass from death to life, and God makes us 'sit together in the heavenly places in Christ Jesus' (*Eph.* 2:6). Then slowly, step by step, we grow in grace and the glory starts to shine in us and from us. On we go, week after week, year after year, 'being transformed . . . from glory to glory' (2 *Cor.* 3:18) into the image of Jesus Christ. We see God's glory in each other's faces and that is heaven coming down to earth and the glory spreading. When we die our souls immediately pass into heaven, into glory.

Then Jesus will come again in the clouds of heaven. We will be raised, and our bodies will be changed, transformed and glorious. The whole created universe will be renewed when God by Christ will reconcile all things to himself. All the effects of sin will be removed and everything Satan has done will be cancelled. The New Jerusalem will come down from God out of heaven to earth, and there will be a new heaven and a new earth: one marvellous reality filled with the radiance of God, pulsating with his immediate presence and transcendent glory. God's glory will be fully restored.

Listen to Jonathan Edwards:

> In the creature's knowing, esteeming, loving, rejoicing in and praising God the glory of God is exhibited and acknowledged . . . The beams of glory come from God, are something of God, and are refunded back again to their original. So that the whole is of God, and in God, and to God; and he is the beginning, and the middle, and the end.[1]

[1] *Works, Vol. 1,* p. 120.

Heaven is created for God's glory. It is the place where his glory is most fully known.

OUR PERSPECTIVE ON HEAVEN

What we have said so far should serve to remind us that heaven does not exist primarily for our sake. Its main purpose is not to make us happy, to offer us a selection of pleasures, or to provide for us an eternity of well-being. It will do all these things, as we shall see; but that is not why God created heaven and it is not why he will bring heaven to its glorious consummation at the return of Christ. Heaven exists for God's own glory.

It is essential that this be absolutely clear before we move on. If it is not, our whole concept of heaven will be poisoned by self-centredness. We will have a degraded perspective, interested in heaven only for what we hope to get out of it. And that is profoundly wrong. On a radio discussion recently the panellists, all well-known, were asked about heaven. Unusually enough, they all believed in heaven and expected to go there. But not one person mentioned the existence of God. He was irrelevant. That same notion – 'What's in it for me?' – may be present in many of us without our even realizing it.

Yet we have to dismiss any such ideas from our minds as utterly unworthy. It is for God's glory that heaven exists. In fact, in the Bible, 'heaven' and 'God' are sometimes used interchangeably. The prodigal son told his father, 'I have sinned against heaven and in your sight' (*Luke* 15:21), meaning that, as well as dishonouring his father, he had sinned against God. When Matthew speaks of the 'kingdom of heaven' he is referring to the kingdom of God. Heaven exists for God, and apart from God it has no meaning. We must never, not for a moment, think of heaven apart from him. We will be sane and safe and biblical in our studies only if right at the forefront of our thinking is this concept: heaven is for God and his glory.

How does this strike you? As somewhat remote? Too theoretical? Here is a valuable test of your spiritual state. You are eager to hear about what you will enjoy in heaven, its pleasures and delights. God and his glory do not concern you so much. But think for a moment. If you are not interested in God's glory, you are not interested in the reason for which this universe was made. You are not interested in the most important reality there is. You need to fall down before God and confess your blindness: 'O Lord God, I am so insensitive to you that I don't even care about the most important thing in the universe. I am ashamed and sorry that the thought of your glory does not captivate me as it should. Forgive me my sinfulness. Give me a renewed heart and a fresh perspective, I pray'.

THE PRESENCE OF HEAVEN

If you are a believer, does thinking of God's glory not thrill you? Does it not fill you with delight to reflect that at this very moment there is a place where his glory is shining perfectly, uninterruptedly, without shadow or blemish? Soldiers have described how, amid the horrors of war, they were comforted by thoughts of home – a place of peace and happiness where their loved ones were safe. To know that home existed, secure and inviolate, strengthened them for the battle. In the same way we can pause in the struggles and disappointments of life and praise God that somewhere, even now, heaven is a reality.

Nor is the glory confined to that unseen realm. We can look at this sin-stained world and rejoice that beams of heaven's glory are coming down and sending out their light more and more in the lives of Christ's people. Since heaven is created for God's glory, it surely follows that we have an advance instalment of heaven wherever God's glory is seen. His saving work in a human heart displays it powerfully. As Matthew Henry says, 'Grace is glory begun'. If you have grace in your heart, then glory is begun in your heart.

And glory can be seen in strange and dreadful places. Suffering can be glorious, and weakness and death. Do you remember our Lord's prayer as he predicted his 'hour' of suffering, his being nailed to the cross? 'Father, glorify your name' (*John* 12:28). Calvary was a demonstration of glory. Peter was told that he would glorify God, and this promise referred not to his miracles or his preaching, but to his death (*John* 21:19). We can see heaven on a hospital bed, in the face of a dying believer. We can see heaven in a faithful Christian, struggling on against difficulties day after day.

In fact, it is our high privilege to begin living the life of heaven here on earth so that people may see heaven in us, for Paul says, 'Whether you eat or drink, or whatever you do, do all to the glory of God' (*1 Cor.* 10:31). We can show heaven where we work, in our homes, or as we sit and worship with our families. We can show heaven by

Christ-like kindness and patience, honesty and meekness. 'Grace is glory begun' and, wherever grace is seen, God's glory is seen and there is heaven.

We may, in measure, live in heaven now, for it is found in any place where we meet with God. After one of the supreme experiences of his life, Jacob exclaimed, 'Surely the Lord is in this place . . . This is none other than the house of God, and this is the gate of heaven!' (*Gen.* 28:16–17). Here on earth we may all experience heaven daily. Wherever we are may truly be the house of God. As you read these words, you may pause and stand within the gate of heaven. Let us pray that God's glory in Christ may so fill our hearts, minds and lives that we may dwell in heaven, now and for ever.

7

The Lamb Is Heaven's Lamp

SOME BIBLICAL DESCRIPTIONS of heaven are rather hard to understand. This is because symbolic language is being used. The realities referred to are so far beyond our experience that God employs metaphors and pictures to convey to us an idea of what heaven will be like. Take, for example, Revelation 21, where 'the holy city, Jerusalem' is portrayed as a massive cube, 1500 miles long, broad and high. 'The city' we are told, 'was made of pure gold, like clear glass' (v. 18). It had twelve gates of pearl, and 'a great and high wall' (v. 12) made of jasper, with twelve foundations 'adorned with all kinds of precious stones' (v. 19). What an intriguing and evocative description! It appeals to our imagination, our sense of beauty and wonder. But we must admit that it is, at the same time, mysterious. Appealing, yes, but not easy to visualize.

Yet the Bible's favourite way of describing heaven is not in the least hard to understand, but so clear that a child can grasp it. In the New Testament, heaven means being with Jesus. On one occasion the Lord is speaking to his troubled disciples, reassuring them about a future which seems uncertain and threatening. How does he do it? With what details about the life to come does he seek to allay their anxieties and keep hope alive in their hearts? 'I will come again', he says 'and receive you to Myself; that where I am there you may be also' (*John* 14:3). It is such a simple yet all-embracing statement. 'In the world to come, you will be with Me', is all that he tells them about heaven. But no more details are necessary, for this is enough. Similarly, in his great high-priestly prayer, he makes a request on behalf of his followers, 'Father, I desire that they also whom You gave Me may be with Me where I am' (*John* 17:24). 'With Me' – here is the fulness of blessing, the sum of glory. The dying robber who has come to faith while hanging on a cross is given the same promise, slightly amplified: 'Today you will be with Me in Paradise' (*Luke* 23:43). The message is plain. 'You will be with Me'. Above and beyond everything else, heaven means being with Jesus.

It is interesting that the New Testament nowhere speaks of believers going 'to heaven' when they die. Instead, they go to be 'with Christ'. Paul writes from prison to the Christians in Philippi, explaining how eager he is for the life to come, 'having a desire to depart' from his present existence. But what, or who, is the attraction in that future realm? Not so much, apparently, heaven itself. The apostle's great desire is 'to depart and be with Christ, which is far better' (*Phil.* 1:23). 'To be absent from the body' is, above all else, 'to be present with the Lord' (2 *Cor.* 4:8). For Paul, heaven means Jesus, so much so that the place and the Person are almost equated. Just as heaven is often synonymous with the glory of God, so is it inextricably identified with the Son of God, in whom his glory is revealed.

Why is being with Christ such a central component of heaven? Why can John say of the Holy City, 'the Lamb is its light', or better, 'its lamp' (*Rev.* 21:23)? Why this emphasis on the association between the Lord Jesus Christ and the world to come? We know that heaven is his home. We know that he came down from heaven to earth and that it was heaven to which he returned after his resurrection. But there must be more to the connection than this. Let us explore several reasons why Christ and heaven are so closely linked.

CHRIST BRINGS US TO HEAVEN

The first reason is that it is Christ who brings us to heaven. This being so, we cannot think of heaven without thinking of the One who is responsible for our being there. The two are inseparable.

The great practical question in all our study of heaven is, how can we, who are sinners, reach this wonderful place? As we shall be reminded later, it is where human happiness is at last made perfect. We have seen already that it is the realm where the Lord's glory shines in brilliant splendour, the dwelling place of God Most High. So it is surely obvious that we can never earn heaven by our merits or reach it by our own efforts. Think of our sins, innumerable and grievous. They disqualify us completely. Heaven is a holy place and nothing that defiles shall ever enter there (*Rev.* 21:27). You and I would pollute it. Think of the dimness and the limitations of our understanding. How could our naked spirits bear the uncreated beam of the presence of God? Finite creatures that we are, we would be annihilated. God's glory would overwhelm us. We would be undone.

How can we suppose that, by trying our very hardest, we could ever become worthy of crossing the chasm between cursed earth and sinless heaven? Yet there is an almost universal idea that humans can deserve everlasting life. This is the working assumption of other religions. It is the incoherent hope of the man in the street. People think that it is somehow natural and fitting that they should go to heaven. They believe, in spite of all the evidence, that they have a right to eternal bliss. If their joyful destiny is questioned, they are hurt and offended. But the merest glimpse of heaven's glory would render any such notion preposterous. We would see in an instant our unworthiness to be there, our utter inability to exist in that holy place. Sooner could a worm aspire to be a brain surgeon than a sinner expect to work his own passage to glory. In and of ourselves, there is no hope that we shall ever reach heaven, no matter what we do, no matter how energetically and persistently we strive. It will never happen! There is only one way, and that is through the Lord Jesus Christ. He says, 'I am the way, the truth and the life. No one comes to the Father except through Me' (*John* 14:6). He is the only possible avenue by which we may enter heaven.

We know how he brings us there. He redeems us through his death. He came to earth so that those who believe in him should not perish, but have everlasting life. He is the Lamb of God who takes away the sin of the world. He was punished for our sins in his own body at Calvary, when he paid in full for our transgressions and satisfied the justice of God. Christ's death on the cross unlocked heaven's gates for sinners. 'Heaven', says Richard Baxter 'is the fruit of the blood of the Son of God; yea, the chief fruit.'[1]

[1] *The Saints' Everlasting Rest*, Abridged edition, London, 1842, p. 30.

The Lord Jesus also brings us to heaven by making us holy, equipping us to live eternal life. He has provided for all his people a perfect righteousness. In his sinless humanity he kept God's law flawlessly and the white, spotless robe of his obedience is given to each of us when we believe in him. Now that he is raised and at the Father's right hand he continues to change us by his Spirit. Day by day we grow in grace, coming ever closer in our new natures to the likeness of Christ. Not only have we a right to heaven through his death, we are fitted for heaven by his righteousness.

Thirdly, he brings us to heaven by preserving us on the way by means of his present ministry. This is a neglected doctrine, but we need to realize that none of us could continue for one second in the Christian life unless, moment by moment, the Lord Jesus Christ were interceding for us with the Father in heaven, upholding us by his Spirit. If he were to remove his hand from us, we would fall at once. We sometimes speak about the perseverance of the saints as if this were some innate quality deposited in us, a new steadfastness enabling us to stay strong in faith. But such is not the case. Our perseverance is certain because, for every second of our lives, Jesus holds and guards us. We persevere only because we are being preserved by him.

Our merciful and faithful High Priest is able to help us when we are tempted. We can come boldly to the throne of grace to obtain mercy and find grace to help in time of need. He is able to save to the uttermost those who come to God through him, since he always lives to intercede for them (*Heb.* 2:17,18; 4:16; 7:25). If you are a Christian, he is bringing you to heaven as you read these words. Though Satan may wish to sift you as wheat, the Lord Jesus prays for you, so that your faith will not fail.

Is it not thrilling and encouraging to think of the present ministry of Christ, how he is keeping us and bringing us to heaven? All authority has been given to him. He is king of the universe, head over all things to his church, and so, because he controls everything and everyone, his purposes will inevitably be fulfilled, his work must prove effective. It is certain that every child of God will reach heaven, for he himself says, 'I give them eternal life, and they shall never perish; neither shall anyone snatch them out of My hand' (*John* 10:28).

'Out of My hand'. Note the implication. If you are on a busy street with a small child, whose hand does the holding? Does the child hold your hand or do you hold hers? The answer is obvious. At any moment she might let go and run into the traffic. But you will not release your grip. So you grasp the child's hand firmly in your own and know that she is safe. This is why Asaph, one of the psalmists, was sure that he would reach heaven. It was not that his grasp of God was especially secure, but rather that he himself was being held by the mighty Lord. 'You hold me by my right hand', he said. 'You will guide me with Your counsel, And afterward receive me to glory' (*Psa.* 73:23,24). 'You hold'. Thank God for that second person pronoun. Where would we be if all depended on our holding the Lord? But he holds us. It is Jesus who brings us to heaven.

My father had a friend who was a millionaire. He had not always been a millionaire, for as young men they had both been poor. But, after he became wealthy, their friendship continued. He regarded my father as his best friend, the one man who did not want anything from him, who liked him simply for himself. On one occasion, however, he persuaded my father to accept a gift. It was a holiday, on which he wanted company. In the early 1950s the two men travelled by ocean liner across the Atlantic to the United States, and then throughout that country. It was an unusual journey for those days, the experience of a lifetime. Afterwards, when speaking of that trip, my father would rarely say, 'When I went to America'. It was usually, 'When I was with Noble'. The trip was so completely his friend's gift and provision that he could not think of it without remembering the one who made it possible.

And we should never think of heaven apart from thinking of Jesus, for we owe it utterly and in every conceivable way to him. In Richard Baxter's words, 'So then let "Deserved" be written on the floor of hell, but on the door of heaven and life, "The Free Gift".'[1] How then can we distinguish between gift and Giver? Christ is central because it is Christ alone who brings us to heaven.

CHRIST IS SEEN CLEARLY IN HEAVEN

Secondly, Christ is central in the doctrine of heaven because heaven is where, for the first time, we will see him clearly. As believers, we are at this moment 'in Christ'. Joined to him in an intimate, unbreakable union, we are 'members of His body' (*Eph.* 5:30). But our Christian

[1] *The Saints' Everlasting Rest*, Abridged edition, p. 33.

experience on this earth is far from perfect, and one aspect of its incompleteness is that we do not yet see our Saviour. The New Testament often refers to his present invisibility. 'Faith', we are told, 'is . . . the evidence of things not seen' (*Heb.* 11:1). Peter describes Christ as the one 'whom having not seen you love' (*1 Pet.* 1:8). And the Lord himself promises blessing to 'those who have not seen and yet have believed' (*John* 20:29). We trust in Christ, but we have never seen him.

Sometimes we almost seem to see him. During a crisis or a period of trial we may call to the Lord Jesus in our desperation and feel him come especially close in answer to our prayer. Or when we are moved in worship, when the Spirit of God is working powerfully in our hearts, we can be lifted up into heavenly places and the veil which hides him from us becomes for a moment almost transparent. Samuel Rutherford was thinking of times like this when he wrote, 'When Christ comes he stays not long, but certainly the blowing of his breath upon a poor soul is heaven upon earth.' We may experience these moments, the 'blowing of his breath', but, sadly, all too rarely. We long to see our Lord more clearly and more permanently, to be able to penetrate the cloudiness of faith and gaze upon him without interruption.

In heaven we will behold our Saviour and we will no longer be those 'who have not seen'. Job, one of the earliest figures in the Old Testament, was convinced not only 'that my Redeemer lives', but that 'in my flesh I shall see God' (*Job* 19:25–26). Isaiah promised that 'Your eyes will see the King in his beauty' (*Isa.* 33:17). Paul anticipates a more distinct future vision than present faith affords: 'Now we see in a mirror, dimly, but then face to face' (*1 Cor.* 13:12). And John, in the classic text on this subject, assures us that 'We shall see Him as He is' (*1 John* 3:2). Heaven is where you and I will see Christ fully and clearly for the first time. We shall gaze into his face and look upon his matchless beauty.

What does it mean to you to know that you will see your glorified Saviour? Does it awaken a pang of longing in your heart? It will be an awesome experience. John was the beloved disciple, Jesus' closest earthly friend. He knew the Lord well, lay on his breast, confided in him without reserve. Yet when he saw his Master in heaven, he 'fell at His feet as dead' (*Rev.* 1:17). With Peter and James he had caught an earlier glimpse of the glory, and Peter spoke for them all when he said, 'Lord, it is good for us to be here' (*Matt.* 17:4). Will we say the same when we see the King? How 'good' will we perceive it to be?

Our Lord wants us to see him, for he prayed, 'Father I desire that they also whom You gave Me may be with Me where I am, that they may behold My glory which You have given Me' (*John* 17:24). He is expressing a touchingly natural human desire, for we want our friends and family to see us at our best. When we accomplish something or receive an award, we like them to be there. Children's enjoyment in being given prizes for school work or competing on sports day is heightened when they know that their parents are watching. So here it is almost as if the Lord Jesus is saying, 'Father there is so much of me that my disciples have never seen. I long for them to see me at my best. I want to show them who I really am. I want you to show them all my glory.'

And when we see our Saviour, we will be overwhelmed with love, admiration and worship. We will cry out adoringly, 'Your voice is sweet and your face is lovely . . . My beloved is . . . Chief among ten thousand . . . He is altogether lovely' (*Song of Sol.* 2:14; 5:10, 16). Believers have already seen something of Christ's beauty. To us even now he is 'fairer than the sons of men' (*Psa.* 45:2). But we have seen nothing in comparison with what we will discover of all his loveliness and glory, and we will be filled with gratitude and wonder. John Bunyan's Mr Standfast, just before he dies, rejoices that, 'I am going now to see that Head that was crowned with thorns and that face that was spat upon for me. I have formerly lived by hearsay and faith, but now I go where I shall live by sight and shall be with him in whose company I delight myself.'

In a famous illustration, Samuel Rutherford compares our experience in heaven with a bride's delight on her wedding day. What is it that thrills her most of all? Her dress? The flowers? The guests? None of these. 'The bride taketh not, by a thousand degrees, so much delight in her wedding garment as she doth in her bridegroom; so we, in the life to come . . . shall not be so much affected with the glory that goeth about us, as with the bridegroom's joyful face and presence.'[1] This is why the Bible, when it tells us about heaven, tells us about Christ. He is our hearts' desire. It is he whom we long to see there.

[1] Letter 21 in the Andrew Bonar edition of *Rutherford's Letters*.

CHRIST, THE HEART OF HEAVEN'S BLESSINGS

But, once we have entered heaven, what then? We will be grateful, of course, that Christ has brought us to heaven. To see him for ourselves will be joy beyond words. But what happens after that? Will we turn away to something else? Is it possible that, having thanked Christ and admired him, we will be ready to move on to other things, leaving him behind and devoting ourselves to exploring all the wonders that heaven contains? Once saved, will we finish with the Saviour?

Never! It is unthinkable. For Christ is at the heart of all heaven's blessings. To understand this, we must step for a moment into the realm of covenant theology. That may seem an intimidating term, but it is essentially a straightforward and thrilling truth. The covenant is the means through which God brings his people to heaven and at the heart of the covenant is the idea of a Representative. God deals with human beings through a covenant head, a mediator, someone who acts on our behalf.

One of the most brilliant illustrations of covenant theology is that used by the Puritan divine Thomas Goodwin. In his exposition entitled *Christ Set Forth,* he explains that 'Adam was reckoned as a common public person, not standing singly or alone for himself, but as representing all mankind to come of him'. In this he was a type of Christ, who is also a representative figure. This is why the apostle Paul, in 1 Corinthians 15:47, speaks of Adam and Christ as 'the first man' and 'the second Man' respectively. 'He speaks of them', says Goodwin, 'as if there had never been any more men in the world, nor were ever to be for time to come, except these two. And why? but because these two between them had all the rest of the sons of men hanging at their girdle.'[1]

Can you visualize the picture which Goodwin draws for us? He imagines two great giants, one called Adam and the other Christ. Each is wearing an enormous leather 'girdle' or belt with millions of little hooks on it. You and I, and all humanity, are hanging either at Adam's belt or at Christ's belt. There is no third option, no other place for us. And God deals with us only through Adam or through Christ. If you are hanging at Adam's belt, you share in the experience of sinful, fallen Adam, and your entire relationship with God is

---

[1] Goodwin's *Works*, James Nichol edition, 1862, Vol. 4, p. 31.

through him. But if you are hanging at Christ's belt, all God's dealings with you are through Christ. When you received Jesus as your Saviour, you were involved in a massive and momentous transfer. The Almighty himself unhooked you from Adam's belt and hooked you on to Christ's. So you now have a different Head, a different Mediator, a new Representative. You have passed from Adam into Christ, and whereas God formerly dealt with you only through Adam, he now deals with you only through his Son. You are in Christ unchangeably and for ever.

This union with Christ underlies every part of the Christian life. It is why a true believer can never fall away permanently from faith. How could someone hanging on Christ's belt become detached and be lost? It is at the heart of our growth in holiness, for sanctification is based on union with Christ in his death and resurrection. Such is Paul's argument in Romans 6: 'You died with Christ, and you have been raised with him. You are no longer in Adam. Live accordingly'. Why do God's people suffer in this world? Because of our union with Christ. As Paul puts it, 'The sufferings of Christ abound in us' (2 Cor. 1:5). Death itself, that brutal divider of soul from body, cannot threaten our union with the Lord, for believers 'have fallen asleep in Christ' (1 Cor. 15:18). Afterwards, what is the source of our resurrection? Christ, who 'has become the first-fruits of those who have fallen asleep' (1 Cor. 15:20). Our union with Christ is absolutely fundamental to all of this. Every prayer we pray and every answer we receive is through Jesus Christ. Every blessing God grants and all the forgiveness we obtain come through Christ alone. He is our only avenue of approach to God.

Now, will this union be ended in heaven? Is the Father going to break that bond and turn us loose from the Saviour? Is he likely to say, 'Well, it was important for you to be in Christ while you were on earth, but that is now no longer relevant'? To ask the question is to answer it. The Father 'has blessed us with every spiritual blessing in the heavenly places in Christ' (Eph. 1:3). In heaven he will still be our Head, our Mediator, our Representative. God be praised, we will hang for ever from the Saviour's belt. In the words of Thomas Boston, 'Since the union between Christ and the saints is never dissolved, but they continue His members forever; and the members cannot draw their life but from their head . . . therefore Jesus Christ will remain the everlasting bond of union betwixt God and the saints; from whence their eternal life shall spring.'[1]

We will reach heaven only because we are in Christ. But it is equally true that we will remain in heaven only because we are still in Christ. In glory, we will depend on him as much as ever. He will mean even more to us than he does now.

Let us illustrate this point with two further truths.

CHRIST WILL CONTINUE TO REVEAL GOD TO US

We are promised that the pure in heart will see God. But what does it mean to see God? How can we see the One who 'is Spirit' (*John* 4:24)? Certainly there will be in heaven such a new awareness of the divine nature and perfections as we cannot now imagine. Thomas Boston speaks of it as a mental 'seeing': 'Not with their bodily eyes, in respect of which, God is invisible (*1 Tim*.1:17), but with the eyes of their understanding; being blessed with the most perfect, full and clear knowledge of God, and of divine things, which the creature is capable of. This is called the beatific vision, and is the perfection of understanding.'[2] At the heart of the vision will be God the Father, because 'the Son Himself will also be subject to Him who put all things under Him, that God may be all in all' (*1 Cor.* 15:28).

Yet we should not dismiss entirely the idea of a physical seeing. Nor should we divorce the vision of the Father from the presence and Person of the Son. For the evidence seems to point to his continuing ministry as the revealer of the Godhead. In heaven Christ is still the Word, still the Mediator between God and man.

John Owen deals with this issue in his work on spiritual mindedness and his comments are thought-provoking. The beatific vision he defines as 'such an intellectual apprehension of the divine nature and perfections, with ineffable love, as gives the soul the utmost rest and blessedness which its capacities can extend unto'. But such a prospect may seem abstract and intangible to many believers. These things 'are above the capacities of ordinary Christians – they know not how to manage them in their minds, nor exercise their thoughts about them. They cannot reduce them unto present useful-ness'. Yet, he says, 'Scripture gives us another notion of heaven and

---

[1] *Human Nature in Its Fourfold State*, London: Banner of Truth, 1964, p. 453.   [2] *Ibid.*, p. 455.

glory'. Heaven is where faith is turned into sight. 'What then is the principal and present object of faith, into whose room sight must succeed? The infinite, incomprehensible excellencies of the divine nature are not proposed in Scripture as the immediate object of our faith.' Rather, the immediate object of our faith here is the manifestation of those excellencies in Christ. And that faith will be turned into sight. In other words, the object of our faith here will be the object of our sight hereafter. 'The glory of heaven . . . is the full, open, perfect manifestation of the glory of the wisdom, goodness and love of God in Christ.'[1] So, as Christ is the principal revealer of God in heaven, we shall see God supremely in him.

John the apostle tells us that, 'The city had no need of the sun or of the moon to shine in it, for the glory of God illuminated it. The Lamb is its light' (*Rev.* 21:23). The Lamb is the light-bearer, and when we look at the Lamb we see the glory of God. Christ is central in heaven because he reveals God to us. In heaven we will worship God in the full-orbed display of his perfections, especially in the glorious person of his Son.

REDEMPTION IS AT THE HEART OF GLORY

One of the most 'heavenly' parts of Scripture is the book of Revelation and it is full of Christ. A characteristic image of him in that book is as 'the Lamb': 'After these things I looked, and behold, a great multitude which no one could number . . . standing before the throne and before the Lamb . . . Salvation belongs to our God who sits on the throne, and to the Lamb . . . The Lamb who is in the midst of the throne will shepherd them' (*Rev.* 7:9, 10, 17). Christ, the Lamb, is at the centre of all: 'In the midst of the throne and of the four living creatures, and in the midst of the elders, stood a Lamb as though it had been slain' (*Rev.* 5:6). It is he who receives ecstatic worship from the 'ten thousand times ten thousand, and thousands of thousands, saying with a loud voice: "Worthy is the Lamb who was slain to receive power and riches and wisdom and strength and honour and glory and blessing!"' (*Rev.* 5:11, 12).

Why this emphasis on Jesus as the Lamb of God? Because the redemption of sinners is at the heart of glory. God reveals himself

---

[1] *Works,* London: Banner of Truth, 1965, Vol. 7, pp. 336–8.

perfectly in heaven. All his attributes will be displayed in fullness there. But his supreme purpose is 'that in the ages to come He might show the exceeding riches of His grace in His kindness towards us in Christ Jesus' (*Eph.* 2:7). Salvation is what 'angels desire to look into' (*1 Pet.* 1:12) and that, above all, for which they praise the Lord.

This is overwhelming, breathtaking. It makes us want to fall on our knees in astonished worship. The glory of glories in the new heaven and new earth will be the love of God to sinners in Christ Jesus. The frailest, most insignificant believer will one day move angels and the redeemed to everlasting praise for God's grace and mercy. We will look at one another and adore God our Saviour for his matchless kindness. And it will all be in Christ, all because of the Lamb of God who has taken away the sin of the world.

What is almost as wonderful is to reflect on our status in Christ, the astounding heights of blessing to which he will lift us. In heaven we will see the Lord our Saviour, exalted high over all. But that supremacy, that awesome loftiness, will not remove him from us. He will not become One who is distant, ineffably remote. Remember our covenant theology, our union with Christ. We are 'in Him', and in his exaltation we too are exalted.

Have you ever thought of that? You are in Christ for ever. You will always be where he is. His glory will be your glory. That is why he himself says, 'To him who overcomes I will grant to sit with Me on My throne' (*Rev.* 3:21). In Paul's words, we are 'heirs of God and joint heirs with Christ' (*Rom.* 8:17). The devil knew that he was lying when he promised Eve, 'You will be like God' (*Gen.* 3:5). But in fact in one sense he spoke more truly than he could have imagined. The divide between creature and Creator will never be lessened. God will always be God and we will always be the work of his hands. Yet it is a fact that in Christ we are united to the second Person in the Godhead, raised to an astonishing intimacy with the Almighty.

That is why Augustine could dare to say of the disobedience of Adam and Eve, 'O happy sin!' He meant that in Christ the tribes of Adam boast more blessings than their father lost. Believers are raised to greater heights than if man had never sinned, for God has come down to earth, has become one of us and has taken us into himself.

Jesus Christ is at the heart of heaven's glory. We are only at the fringes of grasping what is involved in our being raised and exalted in him. But of this we can be sure: in heaven, he will be – and will remain – more close and more precious to us than ever.

Death Brings Us to Christ

To understand that Christ is central in heaven is of great value for us here and now, for it makes the world to come more comprehensible and attractive. That we will be with Jesus is far and away the most important truth about our future destiny. Paul's approach to comforting the young believers in Thessalonica illustrates this perfectly. They were apparently concerned lest Christian friends who had died would miss the blessings of the Lord's return, and the apostle sets out to reassure them, 'lest you sorrow as others who have no hope' (1 Thess. 4:13).

His description of what will happen is fairly detailed: 'The Lord Himself will descend from heaven with a shout, with the voice of an archangel, and with the trumpet of God. And the dead in Christ will rise first. Then we who are alive and remain shall be caught up together with them in the clouds to meet the Lord in the air' (1 Thess. 4:16, 17). There is almost more information here than we might have expected – the archangel, the trumpet and so on. But, as we anticipate the continuation of the precise description, Paul closes the discussion with a glorious summary: 'And thus we shall always be with the Lord.' Why no further details? Why does he not tell us about heaven? He has. 'With the Lord. Therefore comfort one another with these words' (1 Thess. 4:17, 18). What more information do we need?

And the knowledge that to die is to be 'with the Lord' reassures us about our own dying as well as that of others. Peter Pan, in J. M. Barrie's book of the same name, remarks that, 'To die will be an awfully big adventure.' So it will. The prospect frightens us at times. In our frailty and ignorance heaven can seem mysterious and alien. We are apprehensive about the unknown and find it threatening. But the world to come is not unknown, for it is where we will meet our Saviour.

If you are in Christ, do not be afraid of death. He who has conquered that 'last enemy' is waiting for you on the other side. As soon as our souls pass into glory we will see Jesus. He who has known and loved us from before the beginning of time will welcome us into his immediate presence. We will not feel strange or out of place, but profoundly and permanently at home. We will know that we are where we belong, and everlastingly secure.

WE CAN EXPERIENCE MORE OF HEAVEN ON EARTH

Since heaven means being with Jesus, being with Jesus must mean heaven. And we can be with him now. As Christians, it is our immense privilege to commune with Christ daily, hearing his voice in the Bible, seeking him in prayer, sharing with him our anxieties and concerns, expressing to him our love and worship. We come to Christ with requests for our own needs and those of others and for the advancement of his kingdom. We receive from him direction, strengthening and comfort. Is this not a foretaste of heaven?

Is it not tragic that professed believers have to be cajoled, almost goaded, into worshipping God? The 'quiet time' of personal devotion is neglected by so many, as if it were a tedious burden. Modern Christians are ready to busy themselves in almost any religious activity but that of quiet communion with their Lord, regarded more as a duty than a delight. They hope to go to heaven, claim to be looking forward to it eagerly. Yet the essence of the heaven they profess to long for is that communion with Christ in which they show so little interest!

Something profoundly troubling underlies this spiritual apathy. 'If we do not get to heaven before we die,' said Spurgeon, 'we shall never get there afterwards.' We should spend more time in heaven than we do. We should take greater advantage of the means of grace which God has provided for our benefit, practise the presence of Christ more wholeheartedly, enter ever more fully into communion with him here on earth. The richer and deeper our fellowship with him now, the more heavenly will be our present experience and the better prepared we will be for glory. Isaak Walton wrote of the Puritan Richard Sibbes:

> Of this blest man, let this just praise be given:
> Heaven was in him, before he was in heaven.

That should be true of all of us. We do not have to wait! We can live in the outskirts of heaven today. And how different that would make us! How much does heaven mean to you? Your present relationship with Christ provides the answer.

No One Can Get to Heaven without Christ

But perhaps you are in an altogether different category. You believe that there is such a place as heaven and you want to go there. You are not a Christian. That is to say, you have never repented of your sins and called on Jesus Christ to save you. You have never received him in faith as your Lord. Yet you hope that, somehow, in some way, you will get into heaven.

That is a commonly held hope. But can you not understand now how absurd and groundless it is? We have seen that heaven and Christ are, in many ways, almost synonymous. He is central there, the essence of heaven's glory, the One who has secured heaven for sinners, the One who reveals God in heaven. If he were some peripheral figure in the world to come, it might be possible to conceive of reaching heaven without him. But 'the Lamb is its light' (*Rev.* 21:23).

Can you visualize yourself explaining to God why he should admit you to heaven? 'I had no interest in your beloved Son' you will say. 'I repudiated him, made little of his death, shut my ears to his invitations, disregarded his warnings. Jesus Christ meant – and means – nothing to me. As far as I am concerned, your sending of your Son to earth was unnecessary, a pointless waste. But in other respects I have tried to be a decent person. For some of the time, I have done my best. So I expect you, O God, to allow me into the heaven of the Christ I despised and refused.'

Does the idea of it not make you shudder? Can you not hear how crassly blasphemous such words sound? Yet that is, in essence, the unbeliever's plea, and nothing could be more foolish. Without Christ there is no hope of heaven. So come to him now. Cry to the Saviour of sinners to change and forgive and receive you. If you ask him with all your heart, he will do it, and heaven will be yours.

8

We Shall Be Like Him

I FIRST SPOKE IN PUBLIC, apparently, at the age of two. My mother remembers it vividly. We were having a party of some kind, with grand-parents, aunts and uncles and myself the only child. It was shortly after the end of the Second World War, when food, especially sugar, was still rationed in the United Kingdom and the highlight of the meal, set in the middle of the table, was a plate of iced buns. I was rather slow over my bread and butter, but everyone else, to my dismay, quickly finished theirs and started reaching for the mouth-wateringly sticky pastries. One by one they vanished from the central plate. During a lull in the conversation a shrill, indignant little voice piped up, 'What about me?'

Some of my family make the outrageous claim that nothing much has changed over the years and that the child was truly the father of the man – greedy and selfish to the core. Yet it is not unreasonable for a child, or indeed anyone, to ask, in a variety of circumstances, 'What about me?'

Perhaps we feel like asking this question as we think about heaven. We have learned that it is where God's glory is supremely revealed. We have seen something of the centrality there of the Lord Jesus Christ. But what about me? What about you? What will heaven mean for us?

The apostle Paul is eagerly anticipating the joys of heaven when he writes that 'the sufferings of this present time are not worthy to be compared with the glory which shall be revealed in us' (*Rom.* 8:18). In sharing his delight at this prospect, we can easily overlook the two amazing little words with which his sentence ends – 'in us'. The glory will be revealed 'in us', in you and me and in every one of the people of God. The revelation of glory in heaven will be more extensive than that to be seen in God the Father, Son and Spirit. Believers, redeemed humans, will also be exceedingly glorious. It will be God's glory, of course, not ours. He will confer it upon us and we will merely reflect it. It will not be to our credit in any way. Still, it will be in us that his glory will be revealed.

We want to think now of how glorious we will be in heaven. John, the beloved disciple, gives classic expression to the wonder of our destiny in his first epistle. He recognizes that there is indeed much about our future state which we do not know: 'Beloved, now we are children of God; and it has not yet been revealed what we shall be' (*1 John* 3:2). We instinctively know that to be true. The full dimensions of our heavenly existence have not yet been explained to us, and, if such a revelation had been given, we would not now be able, in any case, to understand it. But in the midst of a delicious incompleteness of knowledge there is one truth of which we can be sure, and so the apostle goes on to make the astonishing statement, 'but we know that when He is revealed, we shall be like Him.' 'What about me, what about us?' We will be like the Lord Jesus Christ, when we see him as he is.

'We shall be like Him'. What does this mean? Let us consider what Christ-likeness involves for our souls in the first place, and then for our bodies.

OUR SOULS MADE PERFECT

'The souls of believers', says the *Shorter Catechism*, 'are at their death made perfect in holiness' (*Answer* 37). That verb is taken from Hebrews 12, where the writer is describing the glorious heavenly company into whose fellowship we enter whenever we engage in worship: 'You have come to . . . the city of the living God, the heavenly Jerusalem . . . to God the Judge of all, to the spirits of just men made perfect, to Jesus . . . ' (*Heb.*12:22–24). Those spirits of just men and women are in God's immediate presence and we are told that they have been 'made perfect'.

It is obvious that such must be the case. Heaven is a place of transcendent purity. 'There shall by no means enter it anything that defiles' (*Rev.* 21:27). The souls of sinful humans would defile heaven and yet we are assured that such souls have entered the glory, which implies that they must have been sanctified completely. Without holiness 'no one will see the Lord' (*Heb.* 12:14) and yet the redeemed do see him. This is possible only because they have been made perfectly holy. The transformation takes place at death, when the soul of the believer goes to be with Christ.

This is an exhilarating truth. God's purpose for his people is 'that we should be holy and without blame before Him in love' (*Eph.* 1:4), and so, as our souls are about to enter his presence, they are purified completely, cleansed from every trace of sin. That is why we are told of the martyrs that 'a white robe was given to each of them' (*Rev.* 6:11). The white robe is a sign of their sinlessness. They 'washed their robes and made them white in the blood of the Lamb' (*Rev.* 7:14).

When we die, our souls will be made perfect in holiness. Let us reflect on that for a moment.

No More Sin

Three one-syllable words, but how much meaning they contain! Suppose that you could wake up tomorrow morning and find no change in the world except this – no more sin. Would things be very different? Of course! The whole planet would be transformed, life in every aspect utterly altered, unrecognizable from what it had previously been. Such is the immense revolution which takes place in every Christian at the moment when our souls leave our bodies and are made perfect in holiness. No more sin. Surely, in the words of Shakespeare's *Hamlet*, that is 'a consummation devoutly to be wished'.

Is it not true that, for the believer, sin is our greatest burden, our deepest sorrow? I have never been able to understand why there should be such confusion over the proper interpretation of chapter seven of Romans. Is it not obvious that Paul is describing our hearts, our daily struggles as Christians? 'The good that I will to do I do not do; but the evil I will not to do, that I practise . . . evil is present with me . . . O wretched man that I am!' (*Rom.* 7:19, 21, 24). Is there anything complicated or unusual about these words? Is this not an all too accurate statement of our frequent sad experience? 'If we say that we have no sin, we deceive ourselves, and the truth is not in us' (*1 John* 1:8).

As the people of God we have been delivered already from much blatant wrong-doing. We are not active thieves or murderers. Our speech is not obviously crude or blasphemous. We lead fairly decent lives. Many of our acquaintances think, perhaps, that we are good people, of admirable character. But we can look into our hearts and we know better.

There is horrible corruption inside the best of us. We are self-centred, impure, impatient, dishonest. We can be cruel to those we know best, snapping at our children, deliberately choosing the words best calculated to hurt our husband or wife, probing viciously for a friend's weak spot, which long intimacy has made us aware of. And, in that momentary loss of temper, we actually want to hurt, we are pleased when we see the look of pain on a loved one's face. When we feel that we have been ill-treated, we can cherish resentment for hours or even days. Sometimes, when we are in the wrong and know it, we are too proud to say the little word, 'Sorry'. Uttering it would choke us. And we are children of God!

Nor are we any better when dealing with the holiest things. We read the Bible and are unmoved by its heart-melting truth. We pray for the lost, because that is our Christian duty, but in reality we care little about them. We pretend to worship the Lord while our minds are on other things, so that, a moment after praising God, we can hardly remember what words we were singing. We are jealous of other Christians. Instead of rejoicing at the graces and gifts God has given them, we are envious and try to tear our brothers and sisters down. Preachers, privileged to proclaim the gospel of salvation, can in the very act of preaching be congratulating themselves on a competent performance. Outwardly we are setting forth the Saviour, but inwardly we are busy grooming our rotten little egos.

It is vile! When we think of it, we are ashamed and hate ourselves. We know that we have been forgiven in Christ. We rejoice in the assurance that his blood keeps on cleansing us from all sin. But there is a wound in our hearts that does not heal, an ache in our daily experience that does not cease to throb. With Paul, each one of us must admit that 'evil is present with me'. 'For my iniquities have gone over my head; like a heavy burden they are too heavy for me. My wounds are foul and festering because of my foolishness. I go mourn-ing all the day long. I groan because of the turmoil of my heart' (*Psa.* 38:4–8).

Until heaven. Until that place where there will be no more sin. Never again will we break any of God's commandments. Never again will we fail our Saviour or cause pain to anyone. Never again will we have to beg forgiveness. God has predestined us 'to be conformed to the image of His Son' (*Rom.* 8:29) and we will be. Sinless perfection is not a fantasy, though we will never achieve it in this life. But in heaven we will be forever free from sin, unchangeably disposed towards what is good. Our prayer, offered so often and with such anguish here, will be fully answered at the last – 'Deliver us from evil'.

Our perfect souls will enjoy a new intimacy of joyful communion with God. We will know for the first time what it means to 'love him with unsinning heart'. There will be no shadow of repentant grief on our souls. Between us and our Lord will be no barrier, no sin, not a cloud between us and him.

Our Sins Are Doomed

Is this not vastly encouraging in our present struggle against our sins? We become so weary of them. Some besetting sin has entwined itself in the fibres of our personality and we cannot seem to get rid of it. There is a particular temptation before which we always fall. In spite of our prayers and resolutions it brings us down time and again. We are conscious of so much in our characters that is grimy and shoddy, not fit to be seen by decent people. At times we are tempted to see ourselves as irremediably flawed and we conclude despairingly that we will never change. We may even have doubted our salvation. But the truth that we will be perfect in heaven is a clarion call to courage and hope. 'Take heart, children of God', it says. 'Those sins of yours are temporary. Their death sentence has been pronounced and they are already doomed. The moment your souls enter heaven they will all cease to exist – blotted out, extinguished, thrown into the depths of the sea'.

The story is told of a thief in Japan who became a Christian. He knew practically nothing about the Bible, but on the first Lord's Day after his conversion he went to a place of worship. All week long he had been wrestling with his life-long habit of stealing. He realized that, as a new creature, he should give it up and yet he was not sure he would be able to. Thieving had been his way of life and he knew no other way to spend his time. How could he change the ingrained behaviour patterns of so many years? On the wall of the church building into which he entered were painted the Ten Commandments. The new convert had never heard of them. But, as he walked in, the first words upon which his eyes fell were, 'You shall not steal'. In his ignorance he did not realize that this was a commandment, but took it instead for a promise. His face filled with gladness and he thanked the Lord in his heart for this assurance that he would be delivered from his sin.

Was he entirely wrong? Is it not true that, in a sense, every one of God's Commandments is also a promise? These laws do, of course, set out the standard at which we are to aim. But they are in addition a thrilling description of what God intends to make of us. The Commandments tell us not only what God requires from us, but what he plans for us and is going to do in us. They are a portrayal of our character in heaven. Once there, we shall have no other gods before the Lord; we shall not take his name in vain; we shall not kill or steal; we shall not bear false witness. In heaven we shall love the Lord our God with all our heart and soul and mind and strength, and we shall love our neighbour as ourselves. We should fall in love with the Commandments. We should embrace them and rejoice in them, keeping always in mind that they are not only our present goal but the blueprint for our destiny. They bear witness to what the Lord will do for us in glory. We will be sinless. What a stimulus to holiness this should be!

PREPARING FOR HEAVEN

If we are about to holiday in a foreign country we make suitable preparation. A visitor to our home the day before we leave would notice the half-packed suitcases, the passports and plane tickets, the guide-books and sun tan lotion. It would not take a genius to conclude that we were planning to travel abroad, for signs of imminent departure would be everywhere. In the same way it should be obvious to those who visit our lives that we are preparing to move, to live elsewhere. Is that the case? Can our friends see evidence in our daily behaviour that we are preparing for heaven? Is it plain that we are not planning to settle down on earth, but have a more glorious destination in view?

An important way to prepare for heaven is to declare war on sin. It is alien to our new nature, grotesquely inappropriate in light of our destiny. We have died with Christ and been raised in him to newness of life. An awareness of this should influence us profoundly. Why do we degrade ourselves, why deny our identity by fooling around with sin? In the words of the apostle, 'everyone who has this hope in Him purifies himself, even as He is pure' (*1 John* 3:3). The hope of heaven leads inevitably to the pursuit of holiness. As Lenski comments, 'There is no exception. He who stops purifying himself has dropped this hope from his heart.'[1]

Our whole way of life should be dominated by the anticipation of heaven. It should affect our activities and ambitions, our recreation and friendships, the way we spend our money and our strength. Earthly life at its longest is a short enough time to prepare for eternity.

In particular, the consciousness of a sinless future helps us to face death without fear, for we know that it means being 'with Christ, which is far better' (*Phil.* 1:23). We should make a habit of picturing our souls in glory, remembering that, for those for whom 'to live is Christ', 'to die is gain' (*Phil.* 1:21). In the words of an old commentator, 'To live, Christ, to die, more Christ'. This joyful realization draws the sting from our last enemy.

And it comforts us regarding our loved ones who have entered heaven before us and who, at this very moment, are rejoicing in the presence of the Lord Jesus. We cannot escape the pain of bereavement. We sorrow, often agonizingly, but not 'as others who have no hope' (*1 Thess.* 4:13). Think of them in glory now. Try to imagine the ecstasy of perfect holiness. If God were to offer to bring them back to you, would you accept? That would be cruel indeed. We mourn their loss, but our grief is swallowed up in a greater joy.

John Bunyan, in *The Pilgrim's Progress*, tells how Christian and Hopeful entered the Celestial City: 'Now I saw in my dream, that

---

[1] R. C. H. Lenski, *Interpretation of 1 & 2 Peter, 1, 2 & 3 John and Jude*, Minneapolis: Augsburg Fortress Publishers, 1930, p. 453.

these two men went in at the Gate; and lo, as they entered, they were transfigured: and they had raiment put on that shone like Gold . . . which when I had seen, I wished myself among them.' Our loved ones are beyond sinning. They are before the face of God for evermore. If we could see them as they are at this moment, we would wish ourselves among them.

Yet all of this, glorious though it is, is incomplete, which is why theologians are right to describe the present existence of believers who have died as 'the intermediate state'. For the dead in Christ have not yet received their full inheritance. They are not yet completely redeemed. Their present condition will change for the better when the final stage of salvation is reached. To this we now turn.

OUR BODIES RAISED IN GLORY

For we will be like Christ not only in that our souls will be made perfect in holiness, but in that our bodies will be raised in glory.

The idea of the immortality of the soul is not distinctively Christian. For many centuries before Jesus, Egyptians, Persians and Greeks shared with the Jews a conviction that there was an immaterial part of man which would never die. Even in our own materialistic age most people have a vague yet persistent belief in an imperishable 'self', a part of us which continues to exist after its separation from the body.

What is peculiar to scriptural faith is the teaching that our bodies also will survive death. In asserting a physical resurrection the Bible is unique and yet many believers have, at best, a tenuous grasp on this doctrine. The blame for such hesitancy rests partly with an ancient Greek philosopher.

Plato (427–347 BC) has influenced human thought in a variety of ways for nearly two-and-a-half thousand years, but in our present context he is significant for the way in which he devalued the material in favour of what is spiritual. Anthony Hoekema explains how, in Plato's teaching, 'The soul is . . . considered a superior substance, inherently indestructible and therefore immortal, whereas the body is of inferior substance, mortal, and doomed for total destruction. Hence the body is thought of as a tomb for the soul, which is really better off without the body.'[1] Plato's memorable slogan,

[1] A. A. Hoekema, *The Bible and the Future*, Grand Rapids, Eerdmans, 1972, p. 87.

soma sema – 'the body a tomb', encapsulated this view. He taught that human beings are immortal souls imprisoned in inferior bodies of flesh. Only that which is spiritual is worthwhile. All that is physical and material will ultimately be left behind, discarded for ever.

Unfortunately this poison of anti-materialism has seeped into Christian thinking, so that many believers are unconscious Platonists. Their views of 'the world', 'the flesh', and even 'the soul' have been distorted by an instinctive hyper-spirituality. Devotional writers look forward to being in glory, because their souls will there be set free at last for worship, unencumbered by the prison-house of the flesh. Evangelists speak about 'souls' being saved, not so often about the redemption of 'people', 'men' or 'women'. But this hyper-spiritualizing betrays a false view of heaven and neglects the fundamental Christian doctrine of the resurrection of the body. It is of the utmost importance that we hold on to the reality of raised and glorified human flesh.

For Plato was quite wrong in claiming that the spiritual alone is good and that what is material is necessarily inferior. The Bible is uncompromisingly against such dualism and we must give full weight to the statement that, 'God saw everything that He had made, and indeed it was very good' (*Gen.*1:31). Matter was good as it came from the hand of God. He did not divide reality into spiritual and material. He made it all, all very good, all of everlasting value.

This is why we are told that the human being is a physical-spiritual unity, not a permanent soul in a temporary body. 'The Lord God formed man of the dust of the ground, and breathed into his nostrils the breath of life; and man became a living being' (*Gen.* 2:7). Man is not his soul. The dust of the ground and the breath of life were brought together to make up who we are.

When God sent his Son to die for us, it was for our bodies as well as our souls. Jesus Christ came to redeem not just 'the breath of life' but 'the dust of the ground'. He bought our bodies by his blood. 'Your body is the temple of the Holy Spirit . . . you were bought at a price; therefore glorify God in your body.' (*1 Cor.* 6:19–20). Note that Paul does not say 'your soul was bought', but 'you were bought'. God is to be glorified in our bodies and, when our salvation is complete, our bodies as well as our souls will be in heaven.

How can we be sure of this? Because we will be in Christ and his body was raised from the dead. About this the New Testament is emphatic, almost shocking in its earthiness. 'Handle Me and see' was Jesus' invitation to his disciples (*Luke* 24:39). 'Take me in your fingers and feel the texture of my skin, the sub-structure of my bones.' John maintains that 'our hands have handled ... the Word of life' (*1 John* 1:1). He was writing to Platonists of a kind, people who did not believe in the incarnation or the resurrection of the body, and his testimony was fleshy and basic: 'I have gripped the Son of God in my own sweaty hands.' The resurrection was as physical as that!

Just as Christ's body was raised from the grave, so will our bodies be raised, 'each one in his own order: Christ the first-fruits, afterward those who are Christ's at His coming' (*1 Cor.* 15:23). This will fulfil God's original purpose, when he said, 'Let Us make man in Our image' and the image was body as well as soul. In heaven that image will be fully restored.

THE SAME, YET DIFFERENT

The resurrection of the body – what a stupendous event that will be in the history of redemption! It will happen simultaneously for all believers at the moment when the Lord comes again. 'We shall all be changed - in a moment, in the twinkling of an eye, at the last trumpet. For the trumpet will sound, and the dead will be raised incorruptible, and we shall be changed' (*1 Cor.* 15:51, 52).

What will our risen bodies be like? We need to be cautious in drawing too close an analogy with the risen body of our Saviour as it is described briefly in the gospels. For, while we will be raised, changed and taken into heaven in an instantaneous experience, this seems to have happened for our Lord in two stages. For forty days after the resurrection his body remained in this space-time universe, still adapted, to some extent, to life on earth. Was there an additional change to his new body at his ascension? Are his hands still pierced? Is his side still scarred (*John* 20:27)? We do not know. But we are sure that, whatever his glorified body is like now, our new bodies will be similar.

They will be the same bodies as those inhabited by our souls on earth. Paul emphasizes that these present bodies of ours, 'mortal' and 'lowly' though they are, will be raised through the Spirit's power.

'He who raised Christ from the dead will also give life to your mortal bodies. We also eagerly wait for the Saviour, the Lord Jesus Christ, who will transform our lowly body' (*Rom.* 8:11; *Phil.* 3:20, 21). God never gives up. As far as his people are concerned, he is unwilling to allow even the smallest triumph to Satan. The bodies with which we were created have been damaged by sin, corrupted by the devil's influence. But God will not abandon them and begin again. He will never allow Satan to boast that he has succeeded in ruining irretrievably at least something for which Christ died, placing our bodies beyond redemptive reach and compelling God to provide replacements. No, God will defeat Satan in every respect and will transform the very body of our mortality and humiliation into something glorious and eternal. Our own bodies – these present bodies – will be transformed.

Yet they will, at the same time, be profoundly different. Paul's analogy is of the sowing of seed, where essential identity is linked with total transformation. Sow a grain of wheat and wheat will be produced, not corn or barley. There is continuity, sameness. But what we notice, the reason in fact for the sowing, is how wonderfully different the new plant is from its parent seed. 'How are the dead raised up? And with what body do they come? . . . What you sow, you do not sow that body that shall be . . . but God gives it a body as He pleases . . . So also is the resurrection of the dead' (*1 Cor.* 15:35, 37, 38, 42). Then, in the fullest scriptural discussion of the nature of the resurrection body, the apostle mentions four key differences between our present body and its glorified future state. Let us look at them in turn.

RAISED IN INCORRUPTION

'The body is sown in corruption, it is raised in incorruption' (*1 Cor.* 15:42). Richard Baxter tells us that he preached 'as never sure to preach again, And as a dying man to dying men.'[1] It is literally true. I am dying as I write these words and you are dying as you read them. Irreversible decay is stealthily weakening us. An inevitable process of deterioration is at work in our bodies, continuing remorselessly moment by moment, until we breathe our last.

[1] Cited in J. I. Packer, *Among God's Giants*, Eastbourne: Crossway, 1991, p. 379.

Something within us protests against this. We feel the urge to 'rage against the dying of the light'. An unbelieving society fears and hates old age and people today go to ridiculous lengths to cling to their vanishing youth. Buying shares in plastic surgery clinics or companies manufacturing vitamin pills or hair-dye would be a financially sound investment nowadays. A family doctor tells me that some of his patients are actually aggrieved over physical ailments, wanting to complain, as it were, to the Manufacturer about the unexpected malfunctioning of an appliance which they expected to be more reliable. Living only for this world, they are pathetically reluctant to accept the fact that their bodies will grow weaker, collapse and die. Nor is this a problem for unbelievers only. If we survive into our middle years, we all begin to experience the disabilities and petty humiliations of ageing, 'When the grinders cease because they are few, and those that look through the windows grow dim' (*Eccles.* 12:3). We recognize our 'corruption' and find it an increasingly unwelcome reality.

But Paul tells us that in heaven no such deterioration will be possible. We will be rejuvenated, for ever beyond the reach of sickness and injury, pain and death. Our present experiences of weakness, frailty and suffering will end. 'Raised in incorruption', no process of change and decay can touch us again.

Raised in Glory

'It is sown in dishonour' (*1 Cor.* 15:43). Part of my calling as a minister involves being present at death beds and seeing the bodies of those who have passed away. What does the coffin contain? A poor, weak shell, no more. The soul has departed, leaving behind the pitiful, decaying flesh of a corpse. It will be placed in the ground to rot. There is no life there, no beauty, nothing wholesome. It is sown in dishonour.

But this same flesh is 'raised in glory'. We do not know exactly what that involves, but it certainly means that in heaven our bodies will be characterized by awesome splendour. 'The righteous', says Jesus, 'will shine forth as the sun in the kingdom of their Father' (*Matt.* 13:43). Wrinkles and grey hairs will be no more, all marks of ageing and weakness will be gone. We will be for ever young, in the beauty of our strength, in bright, God-honouring manhood and womanhood. In C. S. Lewis's words, 'He will make the feeblest and filthiest of us . . . a dazzling, radiant, immortal creature, pulsating all through with such energy and joy and wisdom and love as we cannot now imagine.'[1]

RAISED IN POWER
The body 'is sown in weakness, it is raised in power' (*1 Cor.* 15:43). How weak we are, how easily tired! We lack strength, we become weary, we feel that we cannot cope. 'Chronic fatigue' is an increasingly common ailment in our frantic, burdened society.

But God tells us that in heaven our bodies will be filled with energy. We will not know what weariness is. A new dynamism will possess us, new physical powers, so that the swiftest, strongest Olympic athlete would appear feeble in comparison with a believer in glory. 'Our energies will not flag with fatigue, nor will they be exhausted with age. Without inertia or friction our purposes will be spontaneously executed by inexhaustible energies, to which all exercise will be pleasure, and continuing activity the unshadowed rapture of an immortal life.'[2]

Try for a moment to imagine the sheer physical well-being of heaven. Just as the pains of hell are more excruciating than any conceivable on this earth, so are the pleasures of heaven infinitely more delightful than any we can presently imagine. Our bodies here are subject to the results of the Fall. Even the youngest and strongest do not know what real health is like. We have no idea of the exhilarating sense of well-being that will course through our veins in heaven. It will be physical pleasure of the most intense kind.

RAISED A SPIRITUAL BODY
'It is sown a natural body, it is raised a spiritual body' (*1 Cor.* 15:44). We need to be careful here. 'Spiritual' does not mean 'non-material' or 'non-physical'. That is where many go wrong. It refers, in this context, to a body dominated by the Holy Spirit. The 'spiritual' man (*1 Cor.* 2:15) is indwelt and directed by the Spirit. 'Spiritual songs' (*Eph.* 5:19) are inspired by the Spirit. In the same way, 'a spiritual body' is one completely under the Spirit's control.

[1] *Mere Christianity,* Collins, 1952, p. 172.
[2] A. A. Hodge, *Evangelical Theology*, 1890, repr. Edinburgh: Banner of Truth, p. 381.

Cornelis P. Venema explains the distinction between 'natural' and 'spiritual' like this: 'These terms do not contrast a body that is made up of "material stuff" with a body that is made up of "spiritual stuff", as if to suggest that the resurrection body will be immaterial or non-fleshly. Rather, they distinguish sharply the present body as one which belongs to the present age which is passing away and under the curse of God, and the resurrection body which belongs to the life of the Spirit in the age to come.'[1]

At present, our bodies hinder us in our Christian living. They hunger, lust and grow tired. Their demands can distract and divert us from God. But not in heaven. There, our bodies will help us as the obedient servants of our spirits. 'Our wills will not be confined to indirect and difficult action through cumbrous machinery, but the whole soul will act directly upon every subservient force.'[2] Body and soul together will enable us to worship and serve the Lord.

This is the glory which will be revealed in us. Our souls will be sinless, perfect. Our bodies will be incorruptible, glorious, powerful, Spirit-filled. We will be like our Saviour, conformed to his image. The angels will look at us and glorify God. Is it not thrilling to think of what our Father is going to make of us, what riches of blessing he plans to shower upon us?

OUR LORD'S DELIGHT IN US

Yet what is even more amazing is that our Lord and Saviour will himself be thrilled as he looks at us in heaven. Gazing upon his people, he will be filled with affection and delight. 'He shall see the labour of His soul, and be satisfied' (*Isa.* 53:11).

That will be true of his redemptive work in general. Christ will see all his sheep safely gathered in, every one of the elect in glory. There will be no empty spaces, no one missing or lost. He will feel no sense of incompleteness or regret. He will be satisfied with the results of the labour of his soul.

But the Lord Jesus will also be satisfied with each of us individually. We may find that hard to believe, because we are far from satisfied with ourselves. All too aware of our weaknesses and

---

[1] *The Promise of the Future*, Edinburgh: Banner of Truth, 2000, p. 374.
[2] A. A Hodge, *Evangelical Theology*, p. 381.

limitations, we are often discouraged with ourselves, ashamed of what we are. We do not see ourselves as loveable, so how could Christ love us? A nagging fear enters our minds that, although he will be gracious and kind as he welcomes us into heaven, he will at the same time feel a distinct sense of disappointment. We may not be what he hoped for.

We need not be afraid, for we will by then be changed, conformed to his likeness. God's work of grace in each and all of us will have been brought to such a pitch of perfection that the Lord will be ravished with love for his bride, 'a glorious church, not having spot or wrinkle or any such thing' (*Eph.* 5:27). We will be all he wants, everything he desires. We will be the people he chooses to be with him for ever. 'Behold, you are fair, my love!' he will exclaim (*Song of Sol.* 1:15). We will then be able to say with joyful assurance, 'Jesus loves me, this I know.' That will be heaven.

It is himself that Christ will see in us, himself that he will love in us. That is why we are promised that 'we shall be like Him' (*1 John* 3:2). For it is nothing other than his own holy beauty that he will admire.

9
Fullness of Joy

JOHN BUNYAN WAS ONCE BEING PESTERED by a sceptic who kept asking
him silly, unanswerable questions about heaven in the hope of
making Christianity appear ridiculous. The Puritan pastor eventually
transmuted his irritation into good advice by telling his questioner to
trust Christ and live a holy life so that he could go to heaven and find
out the answers for himself. The Bible is written to enable us to do
just that. It is not meant to satisfy our curiosity but to call us to faith.
Much about heaven that we might like to know is not revealed in
Scripture, but this is not because the human writers were incompetent,
trying to describe heaven and failing. It is rather because their purpose
was evangelistic and pastoral. Scripture reveals to us all about heaven
that we need to know at present.

We are told, above all, that it is a place of happiness. David was
sure of this when he wrote, 'I have set the LORD always before me . . .
therefore my heart is glad . . . my flesh also will rest in hope . . . You
will show me the path of life; in Your presence is fullness of joy; at
Your right hand are pleasures forevermore' (*Psa.* 16:8–9, 11). This
magnificent affirmation could stand as the confession of faith of all
Old and New Testament believers. It is still a central Christian
conviction. 'Fullness of joy.' We believe it and look forward to it with
all our hearts.

But can we be a little more specific? God our Father understands our natural curiosity, our eagerness to know about the life to come, and so he has provided us with a considerable amount of information about it. In this closing study we consider the environment in which we will live, our relationships with redeemed fellow human beings and how we will be occupied there.

THE NEW HEAVEN AND THE NEW EARTH

We have seen already that heaven can seem intangible and elusive. It is hard for us to imagine what life there will be like and this uncertainty may mean that we do not long for it as much as we should. We know that we will be with Christ and will see God in his glory. So why are we not more excited at the prospect? Why can we not say in all honesty with Paul that we 'desire to depart' (*Phil.* 1:23)? Why are we willing, more often than not, for our entry into heaven to be postponed indefinitely? Part of the problem is certainly our spiritual insensitivity, but are there other reasons why heaven seems to hover just beyond the horizon of our understanding and our desire?

Our lack of interest may be due in part to the fact that the Bible so often speaks of heaven in what might appear to be negative terms. It tells us what heaven is not like: there will be no sin, no sorrow, no pain, no night, no death (*Rev.* 21:4, 27; 22:5). Peter's classic description is similarly expressed when he writes of the 'inheritance incorruptible and undefiled and that does not fade away, reserved in heaven for you' (*1 Pet.* 1:4). He does not tell us directly what heaven is like, but describes it by listing the disadvantages from which it is free.

Now this is perfectly appropriate language for anything that is wonderful beyond description. When a young man falls in love, he does not provide his mother with a clinical summary of his beloved's height, weight, body type and distinguishing marks. 'She's just the most amazing girl!', he babbles. 'I've never met anyone like her. She is absolutely indescribable!' That conveys his ardour perfectly. It expresses exactly how he feels. But if the young woman were to go missing, it would hardly serve as the basis for a police search. His language provides a vivid impression but is undeniably short on detail.

This is why Scripture pictures heaven as it does. Such language is not negative in the least. It expresses wonder and awe, transcendent amazement and delight. It alerts us to the truth that heaven is thrilling and glorious beyond our comprehension, far beyond the utmost grasp of our powers of speech. But we can all too easily misunderstand the language, miss the glory and become unwarrantably frustrated by the lack of positive detail.

Another difficulty may be with what scholars call the 'enamelled' or 'jewelled' imagery of heaven, the sea of glass, gates of pearl, crowns and streets of gold (*Rev*. 15:2; 21:21; 4:4). These descriptions, of course, are not meant to be taken literally. They are vivid poetic metaphors for a reality which is indestructible, gleaming, incalculably precious. But again we may misread the imagery and be left with the impression of a place which is cold, hard and unnatural. If invited for a walk, most of us would prefer a leafy country lane to a street paved with gold. One is natural and instantly appealing; the other seems lifeless and manufactured. Poor interpretation of Scripture is a serious matter! It can distort glory and weaken our anticipation of the world to come.

But perhaps the greatest obstacle to a true appreciation of heaven is our inability to imagine our bodies there. Though we believe in the resurrection of the body, 'heaven' still brings to mind a realm which is immaterial, not physical in any real sense. We are all too prone to think of a place which is fundamentally unsuitable for physical bodies.

Yet the Bible tells us that heaven is the ideal environment for them. At Christ's second coming this earth, which God created for our habitation and his glory, will be restored and renewed. All traces of sin will be removed from the planet, heaven and earth will come together in a wonderful unity, and 'the earth will be filled with the knowledge of the glory of the LORD, as the waters cover the sea' (*Hab*. 2:14). Commenting on the words 'Behold, the tabernacle of God is with men, and He will dwell with them' (*Rev*. 21:3), A. A. Hoekema states: 'Since where God dwells, there heaven is, we conclude that in the life to come heaven and earth will no longer be separated, as they are now, but will be merged. Believers will therefore continue to be in heaven as they continue to live on the new earth.'[1] But this teaching, plain as it is in Scripture, has been so neglected that it sounds like heresy to some who are hearing it for the first time.

The clearest exposition of it is to be found in the eighth chapter of Romans, where Paul links the destiny of the material creation with

[1] *The Bible and the Future*, p. 285.

that of human beings. He recalls that it was because of man's sin that earth was spoiled, 'For the creation was subjected to futility' (*Rom.* 8:20) when God said to disobedient Adam 'Cursed is the ground for your sake' (*Gen.* 3:17). But this same fallen world will benefit from man's salvation. Just as Adam's sin brought a curse, so will Christ's obedience bring about a blessing. Paul personifies creation, which 'means the animals; it means vegetation, flowers, grass; it means the rivers and the streams, the mountains and the hills; it means the earth itself'.[1] He pictures it standing, as it were, on tip-toe, alive with 'earnest expectation' as it 'eagerly waits for the revealing of the sons of God' (8:19). Why this eager anticipation? 'Because the creation itself also will be delivered from the bondage of corruption into the glorious liberty of the children of God' (8:21).

Something marvellous is going to happen to this earth of ours. Christ speaks of 'the regeneration, when the Son of Man sits on the throne of His glory' (*Matt.* 19:28) and the word 'regeneration' here could almost be translated 'the second genesis'. Peter terms it the 'restoration of all things' (*Acts* 3:21). Everything will be renewed. The earth on which we now live will be gloriously transformed. 'Heaven on earth – that is where we shall spend our eternity. God's plan of redemption is not complete until there is an earth for man to live in and on, in the body.'[2]

This is how God always works in redemption. When our first parents sinned and fell, God did not scrap the human race and start all over again. No, his purpose was to save that very humanity which had been enslaved by sin. When we trust in Christ, God does not provide us with brand new personalities. Instead, by the power of his Spirit, he gradually transforms into the likeness of his Son that which has been damaged. The Church Fathers used to say, 'Grace does not destroy nature, but restores it.' As new creatures in Christ we become more 'natural', more ourselves, than we ever were before. And we have seen in the previous chapter that God will not throw away our present bodies and give us completely new ones. It is these very bodies of ours which he will glorify.

'The continuity between the pre- and post-resurrection body of the believer finds its counterpart in the continuity between the present

---

[1] D. M. Lloyd-Jones, *The Final Perseverance of the Saints, Romans 8:17–39,* Edinburgh: Banner of Truth, p. 49.   [2] *Ibid.*, p. 89.

and the renewed creation.'[1] Just as God is renewing the human race and just as he will glorify the human body, so he is going to restore and glorify this present world. Satan will not have the final say regarding the destiny of our planet. In Robert L. Dabney's words, 'This conclusion gives us a noble view of the immutability of God's purpose of grace, and the glory of His victory over sin and Satan . . . Messiah will come and re-establish His throne in the midst of His scarred and ravaged realm; He will cleanse away every stain of sin and death, and make this earth bloom forever with more than its pristine splendour.'[2]

An awareness of the future renovation of the earth casts a flood of light on many statements of the prophets and the psalmists which we can tend to overlook. Some Christians believe that these prophecies refer to a golden age before Christ's return. But others spiritualize them completely, bleeding them of any material fulfilment and seeing them as no more than pictures of spiritual blessings. Yet there is a literalness here which we should not ignore, for they are telling us what will indeed happen to this present world. 'The wolf also shall dwell with the lamb, The leopard shall lie down with the young goat, The calf and the young lion and the fatling together; And a little child shall lead them' (*Isa.* 11:6). 'The wilderness and the wasteland shall be glad for them, And the desert shall rejoice and blossom as the rose' (*Isa.* 35:1). Creation itself is summoned to gladness at the prospect of its approaching glory: 'Let the heavens rejoice, and let the earth be glad; Let the sea roar, and all its fullness; Let the field be joyful, and all that is in it. Then all the trees of the woods will rejoice before the LORD. For He is coming' (*Psa.* 96:11–13).

When the Lord Jesus said 'Blessed are the meek, For they shall inherit the earth' (*Matt.* 5:5), he meant exactly that. When we pray 'Your will be done on earth as it is in heaven' (*Matt.* 6:10), we are not using an empty form of words or indulging in pious fantasy. Yet do we really mean this prayer as we offer it? Do we expect to see its fulfilment? The day is coming when the will of God will be done all over this earth – perfectly, completely and for ever.

The change will be vast, for 'the elements will melt with fervent heat; both the earth and the works that are in it will be burned up'

[1] Venema, *The Promise of the Future*, p. 377.
[2] *Systematic Theology*, p. 852.

(*2 Pet.* 3:10). Our minds cannot conceive such a cataclysmic transformation, so all-embracing that God can say, 'For behold, I create new heavens and a new earth' (*Isa.* 65:17). But the word 'new' in the ancient Greek translation of this text and in the parallel New Testament passages does not mean absolutely new, but new in quality, in freshness. As with our new resurrection bodies, the basic identity is retained. The cautious A. A. Hodge comments: 'As to the location of the place in which Christ and His glorified spouse will hold their central home throughout eternity, a strong probability is raised that it will be our present Earth, first burned with fire and then gloriously replenished.'[1] Here is the ultimate answer to ecological concerns.

What a prospect this is! Heaven will come down to earth and both together will form one radiant entity, bright with the glory of God. 'I saw a new heaven and a new earth, for the first heaven and the first earth had passed away . . . Then I, John, saw the holy city, new Jerusalem, coming down out of heaven from God . . . I heard a loud voice from heaven saying, "Behold the tabernacle of God is with men, and He will dwell with them."' (*Rev.* 21:1–3). Here is the grand scale of the Father's purpose in the Son, 'that in the dispensation of the fullness of the times He might gather together in one all things in Christ, which are in heaven and which are on earth' (*Eph.* 1:10). Note the 'all things'. Not just the souls and bodies of the elect, but 'all things'. 'For it pleased the Father . . . to reconcile all things to Himself, by Him, whether things on earth or things in heaven' (*Col.* 1:19–20).

Our present world is very beautiful. It is marred by sin of course, not what it once was and not what it will be. But it still declares the glory of God and we can rejoice in its loveliness. We feel a pang of regret at the thought of leaving it, for we all have special places – spectacular views, favourite scenes gilded by memory, the piece of ground which we call home. The beauty of mountains and moors, sea and sky, rivers and forests tugs at our heart-strings.

It is right for us to love the earth which God has provided for us. We are not to love the evil world order, the rebellious world system (*1 John* 2:15). But 'the earth is the Lord's, and all its fullness' (*Psa.* 24:1) and in a very real sense we are not meant to live apart from it, for 'without the glorification of the creation, the glorification of the

---

[1] *The Confession of Faith*, 1869, repr. London: Banner of Truth, 1958, p. 383.

new humanity in Christ would be an isolated and strange event.'[1]
What a joy, then, to realize that we will not have to say a final goodbye
to earth, but will inhabit it for ever in the life to come! We may not
remember it as our previous home, for God tells us about the new
heavens and new earth that 'the former shall not be remembered or
come to mind' (Isa. 65:17), on which J. A. Motyer comments, 'The
awareness will be of a total newness without anything even prompting
a recollection of what used to be.'[2] But surely there will be a deep-
seated sense of familiarity, of belonging. It will not be alien to us, but
we will feel it to be our own place. 'On that new earth we hope to
spend eternity, enjoying its beauties, exploring its resources, and using
its treasures to the glory of God.'[3]

THE HEAVENLY FAMILY

Sartre's comment that 'Hell is other people' is palpably false, for he
meant that hell exists only in the human cruelties of this life. But it is
true that part of the sufferings of hell will consist in the horrible society
of that place. In the same way, a vital element of the joys of heaven
will be the glorious beings in whose company we will live. The
individualism of our age can discolour our view of heaven, leading us
to focus narrowly on ourselves. But the great images in the Bible are
corporate: the holy city, the kingdom which cannot be shaken, the
marriage supper of the Lamb (Rev. 21:2; Heb. 12:28; Rev. 19:9). These
portray heavenly existence as, essentially, life in community, where a
vital part of fullness of joy will be our personal relationships and
interaction.

We have previously considered those relationships which will be
most important – our communion with the Triune God, Father, Son
and Spirit. We will also associate with the holy angels, those bright,
unfallen spirits. How fascinated they will be to learn more about our
redemption (1 Pet. 1:12)! What will we discover about their earthly
ministry on our behalf (Heb. 1:14)? How thrilling to join them in
worship around God's throne!

But our main creature-to-creature relationships will doubtless be
with fellow humans, the elect 'who are written in the Lamb's book of

[1] Venema, *The Promise of the Future*, p. 377.
[2] *The Prophecy of Isaiah*, Leicester: Inter-Varsity Press, 1993, p. 529.
[3] Hoekema, *The Bible and the Future*, p. 274.

life' (*Rev.* 21:27). Let us anticipate for a few moments some of the pleasures of that heavenly fellowship.

WHAT ABOUT OUR UNCONVERTED FRIENDS?
Yet there is a tragic issue which we need to face first. For many will not be there, including some we have known and loved on earth. How will we feel about that? Will it not spoil heaven for us to know that some of our friends are in hell? How can we enjoy the pleasures of glory when a loved one – a mother, husband or sister – is for ever excluded? Every minister has been asked that question in an agony of seriousness.

The answer is clear, but inexpressibly solemn. They will not be our loved ones any more. Our friendship with them will have ended and we will neither miss them nor sorrow over them. The saints in glory praise God for the display of his justice in punishing sin: 'Alleluia! Salvation and glory and honour and power belong to the Lord our God! For true and righteous are His judgments' (*Rev.* 19:1). In the sobering words of Jonathan Edwards, 'The heavenly inhabitants . . . will then be perfectly conformed to God in their wills and affections. They will love what God loves, and that only. However the saints in heaven may have loved the damned while here, especially those of them who were near and dear to them, they will have no love to them hereafter.'[1]

We demonstrate true love for others not by objecting sentimentally to hell but by doing all now within our power to bring them to heaven. Only a friendship which is in Christ will extend beyond this life. If that does not lead us to pray every day and to do everything else we can for the salvation of our unconverted family and friends, what will?

A PERFECT FAMILY
In heaven we will experience perfect family life in the company of our brothers and sisters in Christ, all who by faith in him are children of God the Father. It will, in various ways, be an ideal family.

It will be a large family. On this earth believers are in a minority. We can feel isolated or vulnerable and life is a lonely affair for some. But in heaven we will belong to a huge family, with an immense number

---

[1] *Works*, Vol. 2, p. 209.

of relations. It is a place of 'many mansions' (*John* 14:2) and those who will be saved are 'a great multitude which no one could number' (*Rev.* 7:9). Throughout eternity we will have the joy of meeting millions of brothers and sisters of whose existence we had previously been unaware.

It will be a varied family. The multitude is 'of all nations, tribes, peoples and tongues' (*Rev.* 7:9). We will encounter Christians from every century, nationality and culture. All types of personality will be present. Every kind of experience will be represented. Every believer will tell his or her own story of God's mercy – each one unique. There will be no monotony. Just as God enriched creation with incredible variety, so with his new creation, for his grace is 'manifold' or 'many-coloured' (*1 Pet.* 4:10). We will have the fascination of knowing and learning from so many, all with the family likeness, yet all different.

It will be a united family. There will be no quarrels or squabbles. Theological disputes will have been resolved and personal disagreements will be impossible. There will be no denominations, misunderstandings, ignorance or pride. 'O then, what a blessed society will the family of heaven be, and those peaceful inhabitants of the new Jerusalem, where there is no division, no strangeness, no deceitful friendship, no, not one unkind expression, nor an angry look or thought; but all are one in Christ, who is one with the Father, and all live in the love of Him, who is love itself!'[1] The unity of God's people will be complete and visible. Our Lord's prayer 'that they all may be one' (*John* 17:21) will have been fully answered. We will know, at last, 'How good and how pleasant it is for brethren to dwell together in unity! . . . For there the LORD commanded the blessing – Life for evermore' (*Psa.* 133:1, 3).

It will be an attractive family. There are Christians here whom we try to love but find it hard to like. (Does anyone come immediately to mind?) But there will be no cantankerous family members in heaven, for all believers will be holy and admirable. Their personalities will be radiant with Christ-like beauty. To love such beings will be a joy, not a duty. Being with them will be a thrilling privilege, an inexhaustible delight.

---

[1] *The Saints' Everlasting Rest*, Abridged edition, London, 1842, p. 290–1.

It will be a satisfying family. In this life, we can be badly treated, unappreciated, neglected. Friendship is among the greatest of blessings, but real friends are not always easy to come by. Single Christians wish at times that God had chosen to provide them with a life partner. Many others know the sudden solitariness of bereavement. But in our heavenly family we will have tens of thousands of fulfilling relationships. Earthly loneliness will have been swallowed up in an ocean of truer friends than we have ever previously known. We will be overwhelmed for ever with pure and perfect love. For the first time that well-known phrase will mean exactly what it says: 'One great big happy family'.

Closer Relationships

But what about those who are nearest to us on earth? Will I still have a special relationship with my wife in heaven? Will you still treat your parents as father and mother? Will our close friends here be our close friends there? It is all very well to look forward to meeting tens of thousands. But are we not created in such a way as still to want an inner circle? Such questions are natural, but not easy to answer.

We will certainly know one another in heaven. King David looked forward to being reunited with his dead son there. 'I shall go to him,' he said (2 *Sam.* 12:23). Paul urges bereaved Christians not to 'sorrow as others who have no hope. For . . . God will bring with Him those who sleep in Jesus' (1 *Thess.* 4:13, 14). The reason for not grieving like unbelievers is that their parting is not permanent. They will meet again. We cannot know less in heaven than we did on earth and so we will recognize there those known to us here. That is surely comforting.

We are also told that many aspects of marriage will no longer be appropriate in glory, where 'they neither marry nor are given in marriage' (*Matt.* 22:30). There will be no reproduction. The husband will not need a helper nor the wife someone to cherish her protectively. Children will not require parental care. The relationship between Christ and his church will be so obvious as to render unnecessary a human illustration.

Does this mean, then, that your husband or my best friend will be no more to us than anyone else among the multitudes of the redeemed? I do not think so.

For every good thing will be better in heaven than on earth. If God has given you a Christian husband or wife, parent or child, brother or friend, you can be sure that, whatever the parameters of your future relationship with them may be, the friendship will be closer there than it is now. You will know them more intimately, love them more intensely, delight in them more fully. It is impossible that we should lose anything good in that place where good abounds. We can look at Christians whom we love especially and praise God that we will continue to love them, more and more, for ever and ever.

Richard Baxter strikes a perfect balance between over- and under-valuing our friends: 'When I look in the faces of the precious people of God, and believingly think of that day, what a refreshing thought it is! . . . We must be very careful that in our thoughts we look not for that in the saints which is alone in Christ, nor expect too great a part of our comfort in the enjoyment of them; we are prone enough to this kind of idolatry. But, yet, He who commands us so to love them now, will give us leave to love them then, when Himself has made them much more lovely. I know that Christ is all in all; and that it is the presence of God that makes heaven to be heaven. But yet it much sweetens the thoughts of that place to me that there are there such a multitude of my most dear and precious friends in Christ.'[1]

WHAT A CHALLENGE TO EVANGELIZE!

Paul spoke of his Thessalonian converts as 'our hope . . . joy . . . crown of rejoicing . . . in the presence of our Lord Jesus Christ at His coming' (1 Thess. 2:19). How will we feel when we meet in glory those whom our witness has helped to bring there? Will we regret then the pains we took, the energy we expended, the disappointments we suffered? We will understand what Samuel Rutherford meant when, from prison, he urged his people to receive Christ because, 'Your heaven would be two heavens to me, and the salvation of you all as two salvations to me.' [2] What will it mean to Christian mothers who gave their lives to nurture their children for the Lord? They were

---

[1] Cited in John F. MacArthur, *The Glory of Heaven*, Tain, Ross-shire, Christian Focus, 1996, pp.173–4.
[2] *Letters of Samuel Rutherford*, Edinburgh, Banner of Truth, 1973, p. 111; Letter 225 in the Bonar edition of the *Letters*.

unappreciated in this world, pitied by society as unproductive drudges. But imagine their joy when their children gather round them in heaven and they can say 'Here am I and the children whom God has given me' (*Heb.* 2:13). What better way to 'lay up for yourselves treasures in heaven' (*Matt.* 6:20) than telling the gospel to the lost?

HOW IMPORTANT IT IS TO LOVE EACH OTHER!

In heaven we will love our fellow believers perfectly and for ever. So why can we not love them more now? Why such hellish quarrels between Christians, such misunderstandings, criticism and falling out? 'Is it not enough that all the world is against us, but we must also be against one another? O happy days of persecution, which drove us together in love, whom the sunshine of liberty and prosperity crumbles into dust by our contentions!'[1] What a weapon our disputes provide for Satan! What dishonour they bring to Christ! Let us try to see each other as we will be in glory and treat each other here as we will there.

OUR SERVICE IN HEAVEN

Is 'service' an appropriate word? Is heaven not a place of rest? Most certainly. The writer to the Hebrews assures us that 'there remains . . . a rest for the people of God' (*Heb.* 4:9). We are told that 'Blessed are the dead who die in the Lord . . . that they may rest from their labours' (*Rev.* 14:13). 'Rest', one of the most beautiful words in the English language, has always been an appealing prospect for the hard-pressed and weary.

In heaven we will enjoy a profounder rest than we have ever experienced before. We will have rest from sin - from both its external assaults and its inner promptings. We will rest from grief and suffering, for 'God will wipe away every tear from their eyes; there shall be no more death, nor sorrow, nor crying. There shall be no more pain' (*Rev.* 21:4). No frustration or disappointment will drain away our strength. Never again will we be exhausted by opposition. Doing our duty in a perfect world will not fatigue but energize us.

---

[1] Richard Baxter, *The Saints' Everlasting Rest*, Abridged edition, London, 1842, p. 44.

What a rest this will be! It will mark the complete fulfilment of one of our Saviour's most winsome promises: 'Come to Me, all you who labour and are heavy laden, and I will give you rest' (*Matt.* 11:28).

Yet rest is not the same as idleness. How tedious it would be to spend eternity doing nothing! We were designed for work and would be miserable without it. Even now the weekly Sabbath is not a day of idleness but of joyous activity. So rest in heaven is not an everlasting slump in a celestial deck-chair but the reinvigoration which comes from fulfilling, with our whole beings, the purpose for which we were created and redeemed. 'His servants shall serve Him. They are before the throne of God, and serve Him day and night in His temple' (*Rev.* 22:3; 7:15). In what ways will we serve God in heaven?

Our service, as the Greek word for 'serve' in the above verses indicates, will be that of worship. Heaven is where God is praised and adored by his creation and the book of Revelation, for example, portrays with incomparable beauty the worship of paradise: 'You are worthy, O Lord, to receive glory and honour and power. You were slain and have redeemed us to God by Your blood. I heard the voice of many angels around the throne, the living creatures and the elders; and the number of them was ten thousand times ten thousand, and thousands of thousands . . . and every creature which is in heaven and on the earth and under the earth and such as are in the sea, and all that are in them, I heard saying, "Blessing and honour and glory and power be to Him who sits on the throne, and to the Lamb, forever and ever!"' (*Rev.* 4:11; 5:9–13).

This worship will take us ever deeper into the knowledge of God. Throughout endless ages we will discover new aspects of his infinite majesty, holiness, power, grace and loveliness. Ecstasy will fill our souls as we learn more and more of his being and ways. We will study all that our Lord has done, the interweaving of his purposes, how the movement of every atom since creation, the fall of every leaf and flight of every sparrow, together contribute to his glory. As this is increasingly revealed to us we will be lost in wonder, love and praise.

We should devote more attention than we do to our worship here on earth. We should seek the Spirit's enabling as we pour ourselves into it, practising now what we shall be doing in glory for ever.

But we must not define worship too narrowly, for our entire existence will be worship. Heaven, as we have seen, will be a physical as well as a spiritual reality, 'a new heaven and a new earth' (*Rev.* 21:1). We will be stewards of this new earth, managing it for God's glory. The writer to the Hebrews quotes Psalm 8 in reminding us that God made man ruler of the earth (*Heb.* 2:7–8). This position of authority, diminished by the Fall, has not yet been restored fully, for 'now we do not yet see all things put under him. But we see Jesus ... crowned with glory and honour' (*Heb.* 2:8–9). The implication is clear. We do not yet see all things put under man, but we will. Because Jesus has gone before us on our behalf and the day is coming when complete stewardship of creation will be returned to us and we will sing the psalm with new meaning: 'What is man that You are mindful of him ... You have made him to have dominion over the works of Your hands; You have put all things under his feet ... O LORD, our Lord, How excellent is Your name in all the earth!' (*Psa.* 8:4, 6, 9).

In this new world we will be given remarkable new tasks. Thrilling avenues of service will open before us, calling for the use of all our gifts and talents, many unsuspected or undeveloped in our present existence. 'The reason, the intellectual curiosity, the imagination, the aesthetic instincts, the holy affections, the social affinities, the inexhaustible resources of strength and power native to the human soul, must all find in heaven exercise and satisfaction.'[1] Throughout eternity we will live full, truly human lives, exploring and managing God's creation to his glory. Fascinating vistas will unfold before us as we learn to serve God in a renewed universe. 'Every legitimate activity of (new) creaturely life will be included within the life of worship of God's people.'[2]

It is challenging to reflect that the greater our faithfulness now, the more extensive and fulfilling our heavenly responsibilities will be. 'Well done, good and faithful servant; you have been faithful over a few things, I will make you ruler over many things' (*Matt.* 25:23). Christ rewards us for work well done by entrusting more responsibility to us.

---

[1] A. A. Hodge, *Evangelical Theology*, p. 400.
[2] Venema, *The Promise of the Future*, p. 478.

But will it not spoil our joy if some are given greater rewards than others? Might we not feel jealous or deprived as we see other saints honoured above ourselves? Not in the least. Heaven is a place of perfect love where, for the first time, we will truly love our neighbours as ourselves. To see their greater blessings will bring us nothing but happiness. What true parent is ever resentful when surpassed by one of his or her children? Our pleasure in their success is greater than if the achievement had been our own.

In any case, every one of us will be given as much responsibility and blessing as we are capable of receiving. 'Although there be degrees of glory, yet all shall be filled, and have what they can hold; though some will be able to hold more than others. There will be no want to any of them; all shall be fully satisfied, and perfectly blessed in the full enjoyment of divine goodness, according to their enlarged capacities. As when bottles of different sizes are filled, some contain more, others less; yet all of them have what they can contain.'[1] What we ought to do now is, by growth in grace and devoted service, to increase our capacity for future blessing.

MADE FOR ETERNITY

The prospect of living for ever in a renewed universe answers the frustration we feel over the brevity of earthly existence. For human beings have always felt that, at its longest, life is still too short. There is so much in this world to discover, such a variety of experiences to enjoy, yet so little time available. How many places there are which we will never visit, books we will never read, great paintings at which we will never look, how much music we will never hear! It is tantalising to see such wealth slipping away from us with every tick of the clock.

How little we know about even our close friends! What untapped reservoirs they are of character and insight! But it would take so long to learn all that we could about them. And what of millions we have never met - their personalities and their stories? We would be enriched beyond measure by their acquaintance. But we never will be – not on this earth.

[1] Thomas Boston, *Human Nature in Its Fourfold State*, p. 478.

In ourselves we are conscious of undeveloped gifts and resources, talents and qualities of which we are only dimly aware. A friend of our family was once asked if he could play the violin. 'I don't know,' he answered, 'I have never tried.' He was being facetious, but in a sense he was right. There is more in each of us than has yet appeared. No one has ever yet seen the real you. We do not even know ourselves properly. But we will not be here long enough for our potential to be uncovered.

After a lifetime of studying the Bible, it is simple realism, not mock humility, to acknowledge that we are still paddling in the shallows of revealed truth. With regard to prayer and communion with God we are the merest beginners. As yet we are novices in Christian living. We want to be better people, kinder and more unselfish, but we wrestle with damaged personalities and are disfigured by the scars of the past. Circumstances have stunted our development. Opportunities afforded to others have never come our way. There is so little time for it all!

Do you feel these frustrations? Do you not hunger ravenously for more and more of life? Does your heart ache at the too swift passage of the years? Is there not a nagging sense of unfulfilment, no matter how happy you may be? Such beings as we are – in such a world – with so little possible!

Praise God for heaven! For every good longing within us is an intimation of immortality, an echo of eternity in our souls, a pointer to everlasting life. We were not created for seventy short years, 'not born for death', in the poet's words. Our Creator did not design beings of such complexity and capacity for a mere handful of decades. 'He has put eternity in their hearts' (*Eccles.* 3:11) and we have not been redeemed to be frustrated. 'Life here is too short, too circumscribed, to be the end for man's marvellous divinely given endowments and aspirations. He scarcely more than gets his preparations made for full and intelligent living until his time comes to leave.'[1]

God has an eternity planned for us to blossom in. Existence in heaven will not be static, but a continual development, for, perfect

---

[1] Loraine Boettner, *Immortality,* Philadelphia:Presbyterian & Reformed, 1956, p. 66.

though we will be, we can still change and grow. The boy Jesus was perfect and yet we are told that he 'increased in wisdom and stature, and in favour with God and men' (*Luke* 2:52). The longings and aspirations of unbelievers will remain unfulfilled for ever, a wasted mockery. But God will bring out in his children all that he has implanted in us, in a universe of unlimited richness and beauty.

Best of all, it will never end. This life is overshadowed by an awareness that nothing lasts, but that shadow will be lifted in heaven. Richard Baxter called eternity 'the crown of crowns'. At moments of utter happiness, a voice inside us whispers, 'I want this to go on for ever.' In heaven it will!

HEAVEN CALLS TO US

Where do we go from here? It all depends on where 'here' is. What is your relationship to heaven?

Are you still outside? Your life so far has been lived in rebellion against God. You have never come to trust in Christ as Saviour. Your sins remain unforgiven and the day of your condemnation is approaching. Yet in the preceding pages you have read a little about heaven's happiness and glory. Do you want to go there? Would it not be a tragedy for you to find out so much about heaven and then miss it at the last? The only door into heaven is the Lord Jesus and that door is still open. Come to him and, through him, enter into eternal life and joy. Why would you refuse? What good reason can you give for rejecting Christ and choosing hell? If you ask him to receive you now, he will. Turn away from sin and death and call on Christ to save you. 'For God so loved the world that He gave His only begotten Son, that whoever believes in Him should not perish but have everlasting life' (*John* 3:16).

Or you may be a believer, needing the present encouragement which heaven affords us. Life can be hard and no fine words will change that. But 'the sufferings of this present time are not worthy to be compared with the glory which shall be revealed in us' (*Rom.* 8:18). Heaven is coming quickly and 'our light affliction, which is but for a moment, is working for us a far more exceeding and eternal weight of glory' (*2 Cor.* 4:17). The greater our troubles now, the greater our glory then. These things will soon pass and we will be with the Lord for ever.

And all of us who are Christ's should live more consistently in the light of heaven. We should be more heavenly minded, for our citizenship is there (*Phil.* 3:20). This doctrine urges us to stop chasing after the little trinkets of this life and to lay up treasures in the world to come. We must not deny by our lives what we profess with our lips.

I hope to meet you in everlasting glory. Till then, may God make us men and women upon whose faces the light of heaven is shining, living in such a way that people will see that we are different. Then we may bring many to heaven with us.

SOME OTHER
BANNER OF TRUTH
TITLES

PETER: EYEWITNESS
OF HIS MAJESTY

Edward Donnelly

A series of studies showing how the grace of God moulded
Peter as a disciple, a preacher and a pastor.

'Heart-warming, challenging, scholarly and comprehensive
is how this book deserves to be described. This work of Ted
Donnelly is worthy of praise on several fronts. It is clearly
written from a pastor's heart for the people of God and for
the servants of Christ in the Church. Whether you are a young
believer in the Lord Jesus Christ or a seasoned veteran in the
ministry of the Word of God, this book has something for
you.'

EVANGELICAL PRESBYTERIAN

ISBN 0 85151 744 7
160 pp. Paperback

THE LAST THINGS
Paul Helm

'This is a quiet, thoughtful, unemphatic book on the great themes of death and judgment, heaven and hell. Written from the broad perspective of Reformed truth, with quotations from Augustine and Jonathan Edwards . . . it is a calm corrective to the excitable "this-worldly" experiential paperbacks of our time . . . I commend a thought-provoking book to thoughtful preachers.'

CHURCH OF ENGLAND NEWSPAPER

'*The Last Things* not only clarifies our view of the future – it also provides a fresher, clearer perspective on the present life.'

MODERN REFORMATION

ISBN 0 85151 544 4
160 pp. Paperback

THE DOCTRINE OF
ENDLESS PUNISHMENT

W. G. T. Shedd

'This classic work by Shedd was first published in America in 1885 in order to resist the growing tide of universalism and annihilationism which was sweeping through parts of Christendom at the time. We are facing a similar problem today and so I welcome the Banner's reprint . . . Hopefully it will challenge Christians to study and embrace the orthodox, biblical doctrine of eternal punishment.'

EVANGELICAL MAGAZINE OF WALES

'An outstanding book, one that every preacher and Bible teacher should have in his personal library.'

BIBLICAL EVANGELIST

ISBN 0 85151 754 4
224 pp. Paperback

THE PROMISE
OF THE FUTURE

Cornelis P. Venema

'Occasionally one reads a new book and feels instinctively that it will become a classic. Here is such a book. The subject is eschatology, the doctrine of the last things. It is a comprehensive treatment, sanely written, thoroughly biblical and spiritually edifying. It is a clear, easy and enjoyable book to read. The language is amazingly non-technical for a modern theological book.'

FREE CHURCH WITNESS

'This is a first-rate book, highly recommended, spiritually very warming and bursting with valuable information and instruction.'

TABERNACLE BOOKSHOP

ISBN 0 85151 793 5
560 pp. Cloth-bound

THE SINFULNESS
OF SIN

Ralph Venning

W e cannot understand the Christian gospel until we know what sin is. Yet modern secular counsellors urge us to ignore both the word and what it tells us about our rebellion against God and his law. Sadly the church too often echoes this cheap and short-sighted wisdom.

First published in the aftermath of the Great Plague of London and entitled *Sin, The Plague of Plagues*, this book gives a crystal-clear explanation of what sin is, why it is so serious, and what we need to do about it. Here is reliable medicine for a fatal epidemic.

ISBN 0 85151 163 5
208 pp. Paperback

HEAVEN ON EARTH

Thomas Brooks

A ssurance of salvation is one of the most important elements in Christian experience. There is no higher privilege than to be a child of God *and to know it*, for assurance brings joy to worship and prayer and provides strength and boldness in witness. Failure and weakness in these areas can often be traced to a lack of assurance. This work, first published in 1654, deals with all these aspects of assurance. 'The being in a state of grace', says Brooks, 'makes a man's condition happy, safe and sure; but the seeing, the knowing of himself to be in such a state is that which renders his life sweet and comfortable. The being in a state of grace will yield a man a heaven hereafter, but the seeing of himself in this state will yield him both a heaven here *and* a heaven hereafter.'

ISBN 0 85151 356 5

320 pp. Paperback